James I

LANCASTER PAMPHLETS

James I

Christopher Durston

London and New York

First published 1993
by Routledge
11 New Fetter Lane, London EC4P 4EE

Simultaneously published in the USA and Canada
by Routledge Inc.
29 West 35th Street, New York, NY 10001

Typeset in 10/12pt Bembo by
Ponting–Green Publishing Services, Chesham, Bucks
Printed in Great Britain by
T. J. Press (Padstow) Ltd, Padstow, Cornwall

British Library Cataloguing in Publication Data
A catalogue record for this book is available from the British Library

Library of Congress Cataloging in Publication Data
Durston, Christopher
James I / Christopher Durston.
p.   cm. – (Lancaster pamphlets)
Includes bibliographical references
1. James I, King of England, 1566–1625
2. Great Britain–History–James I, 1603–1625
I. Title.
II. Series.
DA391.D86   1993
941.06'1'092–dc20   92–44013

ISBN 0–415–07779–6

For my students, past and present, at Strawberry Hill

Contents

Foreword

Lancaster Pamphlets offer concise and up-to-date accounts of major historical topics, primarily for the help of students preparing for Advanced Level examinations, though they should also be of value to those pursuing introductory courses in universities and other institutions of higher education. Without being all-embracing, their aims are to bring some of the central themes or problems confronting students and teachers into sharper focus than the textbook writer can hope to do; to provide the reader with some of the results of recent research which the textbook may not embody; and to stimulate thought about the whole interpretation of the topic under discussion.

Acknowledgements

I should like to thank Susan Doran, who read part of the text, and Jacqueline Eales, Eric Evans, and David King, who read the whole of it, for their helpful suggestions and for pointing out a number of errors and misjudgements. For those that remain I am entirely responsible. I am also grateful to Claire L'Enfant at Routledge for suggesting the project and offering me her support and encouragement.

Chronological table

Introduction: 'a bad king'?

In March 1603, on the death of Queen Elizabeth I and the extinction of the Tudor royal line, the English throne passed to James VI of Scotland, who became James I, the first of the Stuart kings of England. James had by then been king of Scotland for thirty-five years; he had been ruling there in his own right all his adult life and had achieved some considerable success in his dealings with the powerful Scottish church and aristocracy. He had also actively sought the English crown for many years and had manoeuvred skilfully and patiently to achieve the successful outcome of 1603. However, perhaps because he had had to work so hard to achieve it, James seems to have seriously over-valued the prize he had now won. He journeyed south to London in 1603 in the belief that after many years of toiling in a Scottish wilderness, he had at last entered upon his promised land and would now be able to relax and enjoy the abundant milk and honey available in England. The reality that awaited him was quite different. While England did occupy a more elevated position than Scotland in the league table of European powers and possessed the potential to be substantially richer and more prosperous than its northern neighbour, it was also a country racked by acute internal pressures and tensions, and ruled by a crown and government hamstrung by a number of serious and deep-seated structural weaknesses.

During the course of the sixteenth century the English people had experienced a range of new social and economic forces, including a sustained population increase, persistent price inflation, the growth of a new gentry class of middling landowners, and the dramatic expansion of the nation's main urban community, London. They had also been subjected to the sometimes bewildering succession of religious innovations known as the English Reformation. These fundamental and rapid changes had alarmed and alienated many people and created deep divisions which were still very evident in 1603. The English crown meanwhile had entered the new century at war with Spain and desperately short of money, lacking the means to maintain an effective standing army, and dependent on a corrupt and inefficient central bureaucracy and a local administration staffed by unpaid volunteers. To add to James's problems, while Elizabeth had neglected to deal with these difficulties, she had none the less managed to persuade the English people that she had presided over a period of glorious and providential national success, and in so doing had rendered herself a very hard act to follow. James's promised land was in fact something of a poisoned chalice.

James I was to rule England for twenty-two years before giving way to his son Charles in 1625. His record during these years has provoked considerable debate amongst both contemporaries and later writers and historians. The most critical contemporary assessor of James's character and conduct was Sir Anthony Weldon, an English civil servant who had been dismissed by James for writing a highly offensive anti-Scots diatribe following a visit to Scotland with the king in 1617. Weldon's brilliantly scurrilous *The Court and Character of King James* presented James as an unpleasant, unsavoury clown – the infamous 'wisest fool in Christendom' – who was an embarrassment to all those unlucky enough to come into contact with him. It is here that we first encounter the James I who wore heavily quilted clothes to guard against knife attacks, who drank awkwardly because of an over-large tongue, who never washed, and who ogled any handsome young male courtier who came into view. This poisonous piece of literary revenge was to do profound and lasting damage to James's reputation, as it became the prime source for many subsequent historical assessments whose authors failed to make sufficient allowance for its obvious bias.

Weldon's influence is clearly seen, for example, in the work of the early Victorian historian Thomas Macaulay, who accused James of constantly 'stammering, slobbering, shedding unmanly tears, trembling at a drawn sword, and talking in a style alternately of a buffoon and a pedagogue'. Weldon was also of great interest to the popular nineteenth-century Scottish writer, Sir Walter Scott. Scott published a new edition of Weldon's work in Edinburgh in 1811, and later set several of his historical novels at James's court, presenting the king to his wide readership as a gross offender against the moral standards demanded by their own Victorian society. Nor did the rise of academic history in the mid-nineteenth century do much to rescue James from Weldon's malign influence, for the pens of professional historians as diverse as Samuel Rawson Gardiner, Godfrey Davies, Hugh Trevor-Roper, and Wallace Notestein have continued to take their lead from him and to heap scorn and condemnation on the hapless James. The king's reputation reached its nadir in 1956 with the publication of D. H. Willson's *King James VI and I*. While biographers generally need to guard against the temptation to portray their chosen subjects in too favourable a light, Willson had no such problems; he thoroughly disliked and disapproved of James, condemning him for his 'sad irresolution' and 'weaker nature', and dismissing him in his last years as 'a broken, debauched and repulsive old man'.

It is only during the last twenty-five years that historians have belatedly begun to emancipate themselves from Weldon and to present a more balanced picture of James. The re-assessment was launched by historians of James's period of rule in Scotland, such as Gordon Donaldson (1965) and Jenny Wormald (1981). Their researches led them to the conclusion that James VI had been, in Donaldson's words, a ruler 'of very remarkable political ability and sagacity in deciding on policy, and of conspicuous tenacity in having it carried out', and they found it hard to believe that he should have suffered such a serious deterioration in his powers of kingship merely by journeying several hundred miles to the south in 1603. Further investigation revealed that Weldon was almost entirely responsible for James's 'black legend', and that some other contemporaries had left a very different impression of the English king. One of Charles I's bishops, Godfrey Goodman, had argued in his *The Court of*

James I that James had been a 'most just and good king', and Sir Simonds D'Ewes had praised him for 'his augmenting of the liberties of the English'. Another contemporary writer, the royalist historian William Sanderson, had even made an unsuccessful attempt in the 1650s to refute many of Weldon's allegations, and during the same decade Thomas Fuller had commented that: 'the reign of King James was better for one to live under than to write of, consisting of a champion of constant tranquillity without any tumours of trouble to entertain posterity with'.

By the early 1970s the Scottish re-evaluation of James had started to win acceptance among English and American scholars. In 1973, S. J. Houston concluded his short study of James's reign by claiming that he had been 'an exceptional man whose qualities fell sadly short of their highest achievement'; and more recently Maurice Lee (1990) has drawn attention to a number of significant achievements and argued that: 'James's shortcomings were mostly those of style rather than substance.' More fulsome praise still has come from Conrad Russell (1979); after undertaking a detailed investigation of the later parliaments of the reign, he concluded that, like Sir Robert Walpole, James should receive great credit for achieving and maintaining 'a high degree of political stability'. Full rehabilitation may finally be achieved on the publication of the major biography at present being written by Jenny Wormald.

A further complicating factor in all attempts to assess James I's record has been the fate of his son Charles. Charles I was a very different person from his father and during the late 1620s and 1630s he set about ruling in a very different way. Fifteen years into his reign he found himself faced with a political and religious crisis which culminated in a disastrous civil war, his own public execution, and the abolition of the monarchy, the House of Lords, and the established church. Inevitably, those who have studied James's reign have been unable entirely to put aside their knowledge of these cataclysmic events, and have felt compelled to comment about the extent to which James should bear responsibility for them. Writers in the older, hostile historical tradition, who were generally reluctant to point the finger of blame at the tragic figure of Charles, were quick to condemn James as the ruler who, in Gardiner's (1883–4) phrase, 'sowed the seeds of revolution and disaster'. In contrast, those influenced by the more sympathetic, modern approach have stressed that James faced an abundance of dangerous sleeping dogs which he did well to let lie, and have praised him for what did not happen during his reign.

As every generation of historians necessarily recreates the past in the light of its own concerns, any attempt to present definitive conclusions about James I's reign would be doomed to failure. The following pages will attempt only to present a summary of current historical thinking, along with some of the author's own observations on James's record between 1603 and 1625, and on the question of the degree of blame he should accept for the catastrophes that befell his successor.

1

James I: the man

James I succeeded his cousin in 1603 as a result partly of his own lobbying and partly of the principle of hereditary right. Whether he would have been so successful if he had been forced to make a formal application for the post of English monarch is a debatable point. Any hypothetical appointments panel would probably have been impressed with his previous record in Scotland, and he might also have done rather well if asked to give a short presentation on the theory and practice of kingship. On the other hand, the imaginary English selectors might have been put off by his failure to observe the formalities normal on such occasions, and perhaps also by his alien accent and somewhat dishevelled appearance. They would very likely have become rather bored by his tendency to lecture them at length when answering their questions, and, had the selection process involved observing the candidates over dinner, James's lack of refined table manners and over-indulgence in alcohol might have raised disapproving eyebrows. A safer rival – one who more resembled the last English monarch – might well have won the day. The English were, of course, given no such opportunity to vet their new king in 1603, but were obliged to accept James as their ruler along with all his strengths and weaknesses. These would only become apparent to them over the next few years as he faced up to the pressing problems which beset the English crown.

James was 37 years old in 1603, of medium height, with brown hair, a thin beard, and pale blue eyes; he spoke in a thick Scottish accent which many of his new subjects found difficult to decipher. Like all men and women, he possessed a unique and complex personality shaped over many years by a multitude of genetic and environmental influences. Faced with such complexity, historians have too often indulged in crude dissections of James, labelling his qualities as either admirable or discreditable on the basis of their personal moral systems or the accepted values of their day. Those who study the past cannot escape the important but hazardous business of long-distance personality assessment, but they remain on safer and more instructive ground when they avoid moral judgements and confine themselves to classifying personal characteristics according to whether they were an asset or a disadvantage to their possessors in the performance of their public careers. 'Bad' traits after all are often an advantage to those in power, and 'good' ones can prove extremely unhelpful.

An example of the latter case is provided by James's broad-minded intellectual outlook. James appears to have been a man remarkably free from the pull of prejudice and hidebound thinking. By 1603 he had constructed his own idiosyncratic portfolio of beliefs and opinions, some of which were extremely advanced for their time. The ringing denunciation of tobacco smoking in his 1604 *Counterblast to Tobacco*, for example, would win plaudits from the modern medical profession. In later life he expressed grave doubts about the existence of witchcraft – a phenomenon most of his contemporaries accepted without question – and he regarded the English royal custom of touching those suffering from scrofula, or 'the king's evil', as rather ridiculous. Unfortunately, his less independently-minded subjects, who relied upon more conventionally packaged views, often found his ideas puzzling, inconsistent, and contradictory. It was difficult for them to understand how James could be a firm believer in the theory of the divine right of kings and yet very informal in his practical exercising of kingship; how he could oppose Arminian theories on salvation and yet promote Arminians to the episcopal bench; and above all, how, as a staunch doctrinal Calvinist, he could fail to share in the hatred and suspicion of Roman Catholicism and the papacy which were the hallmarks of seventeenth-century Calvinism. As a result, although James's immunity from some of the prejudices which were commonplace amongst his contemporaries may now appear praiseworthy, during his reign it was responsible for creating some considerable misunderstanding and suspicion.

James was not without some personal attributes which were a clear advantage to him in the exercise of his office. Some of these he had inherited; others had been acquired during his long 'apprenticeship' in Scotland. Contemporaries and historians are agreed that, having received an excellent formal education as a child, he was a clever and well-read man, with a deep and genuine interest in intellectual matters, particularly in the areas of kingship and theology. Even Weldon had to concede that James was a *wise* fool, and Maurice Lee (1990) has recently gone so far as to describe him as 'one of the most learned and intellectually curious men ever to sit on any throne'. Furthermore, James was well aware that he was clever and had considerable confidence in his own mental capacities.

Intellectuals do not generally make good politicians, but on numerous occasions both before and after 1603 James's actions revealed that, when he set his mind to it, he was capable of displaying great skill as a political operator. He possessed the flexibility, caution, and patience needed by all successful politicians, but his greatest political asset was his ability to make quick and accurate judgements of individuals and situations. Perhaps because of his aversion to cant and hypocrisy, he was extremely adept at weighing up those with whom he had dealings, and at discerning their underlying drives and motivations. His assessment of William Laud as a man who 'hath a restless spirit and cannot see when things are well, but loves to toss and change and bring things to a pitch of reformation in his own brain', was an especially incisive verdict on a cleric who was to do so much damage during Charles's reign. He was also a discerning political commentator. His remark to Prince Charles and Buckingham in 1624, that by courting popularity in parliament they were making 'a rod with which you will be scourged yourself', soon proved correct. Similarly, his famous 'No bishop, no king' statement made during the Hampton Court conference has too frequently been dismissed as an example of ill-judged petulance by historians who have overlooked the fact that the events of the late 1640s would reveal it to be an all-too-accurate prophecy.

Equally clearly, however, James possessed other qualities which did not help him as a ruler. He was not an industrious person, and he too often left the detail of policy-making to his servants while he himself indulged in his private leisure pursuits. The chief of these was hunting, which took up an enormous amount of his time and often kept him away from London for weeks on end. In 1610, for example, he was absent from the capital, hunting, for much of the time that parliament was debating Salisbury's important fiscal initiative of the Great Contract. This neglect of government was not the result of his indolence alone; it was also a product of his belief that he had worked hard enough in Scotland before 1603 and now deserved to enjoy himself, and of his sometimes misplaced confidence in his ability to stay abreast of complex political developments even when he was otherwise engaged.

While James was reported to have been a courageous, even reckless, horseman, he was extremely afraid of all forms of violence and very uneasy when in the presence of knives or other drawn weapons. He also lived in constant fear of assassination, wearing especially thick clothes to protect himself from knife attacks, and on occasion piling furniture up against the door of his bedchamber before sleeping. The thought of going to war filled him with alarm, and amongst the advice he gave his son in his book *Basilikon Doron* was the suggestion that if he were ever forced to lead troops into battle he should wear light armour to make it easier to run away. The fact that he found funerals disturbing suggests that he may also have had a morbid fear of death. Historians can only speculate about the roots of these anxieties, but, as his mother's envoy pointed out in 1584, he had certainly been 'nurtured in fear'. During his childhood in Scotland he had been subjected to frequent plots and kidnappings, and these 'ruffles' must have left their psychological mark, as perhaps did his knowledge of the dramatic blowing-up of his father, Henry Lord Darnley, in 1567. It is also interesting to note that Mary Queen of Scots was heavily pregnant with James when her confidant and secretary, David Riccio, was knifed to death in her presence. Historians have generally expressed doubts about whether this incident could have caused some pre-natal shock which had a lasting impact upon James, but modern psychology would not dismiss such a possibility, and, if there was no connection, his later aversion to knives remains an extreme coincidence. While James was in a somewhat safer environment in England, the Gunpowder Plot of 1605 and his awareness of the persistent rumours of a conspiracy to massacre his hated Scottish entourage could have done little for his peace of mind. Whatever the reasons behind them, these neurotic fears left James wide open to accusations of cowardice, a quality considered highly inappropriate in the chief defender of the state.

Another, and probably more damaging, facet of James's personality was his large appetite for love and affection combined with a deep self-doubt about his capacity to elicit these emotions. Although he possessed a high opinion of his intellectual abilities, he seems to have harboured real misgivings about his ability to inspire genuine love and affection in those around him. This lack of confidence, which may have been the product of a childhood spent without the normal sources of affection and intimacy, had several regrettable consequences. Because it led James to try to buy affection and made him reluctant to refuse any requests for favour, it was a major contributory factor in his lavish expenditure on gifts and pensions. It also left him extremely vulnerable to the charms of attractive individuals like Esme Stuart and George Villiers who appeared to care for him, and highly susceptible to flattery. This last trait was especially unfortunate as during the course of Elizabeth's reign sycophantic displays of devotion to their monarch had become something of a speciality of the English people. One of the Scottish courtiers who witnessed some early examples of this when accompanying James south in 1603 had warned of the danger that 'this people will spoil a good king'. Jenny Wormald (1983) has also recently argued that James 'enjoyed and had his head turned' by the 'cult of adoration' which he inherited from his predecessor.

James's eagerness to amass evidence of his popularity was also to blame for a number of misunderstandings that developed between himself and his subjects. The earliest of these occurred at the very beginning of the reign. As he journeyed south to London in 1603 his progress was marked by a number of spontaneous outbursts of celebration. Those who took part in these were in the main giving expression to their intense relief that the succession had passed off without serious upheaval. James, however, was much affected by what he interpreted as evidence of his new subjects' great warmth and affection for him. A year later he declared to his first House of Commons:

> Shall it ever be blotted out of my mind how at my first entry into this kingdom, the people of all sorts rid and ran, nay rather flew to meet me; their eyes flaming nothing but sparkles of affection, their mouths and tongues uttering nothing but sounds of joy, their hands, feet and all the rest of their members in their gestures discovering a passionate longing and earnestness to meet and embrace their new sovereign.

Such a misreading of events by one who was normally very perceptive was caused not, as Alan Smith (1973) has argued, by James's 'incurable self-conceit', but rather by a self-*deceit* arising from deep insecurity and an abiding need for reassurance.

Another of James's attributes which proved disadvantageous to him as king was his apparent homosexuality. There is no doubt that James felt a strong physical and emotional attraction towards good-looking men, or that he was eager to surround himself with handsome male courtiers, some of whom he fell deeply in love with. This created problems not only because numbers of his subjects found his public displays of affection towards these men distasteful, but also because, unlike a mistress who would have been prevented by her gender from assuming an inordinate prominence at court, James's famous male lover, George Villiers, duke of Buckingham, was able to use his hold over James to acquire enormous power in the last years of the reign. The exact nature of any sexual relations between James and his male favourites is, perhaps not surprisingly, difficult to establish. Villiers' biographer, Roger Lockyer (1981), has uncovered evidence which he contends proves that some form of sexual relationship existed between the king and Buckingham. In one of his letters to James, Villiers reminded the king about a visit they had made to Farnham in Surrey during which 'the bed's head could not be found between master and dog'. Despite the evidence of this letter, Maurice Lee (1990) remains doubtful about whether a sexual relationship existed, claiming that James was not particularly interested in physical sex. This latter argument may in turn be rather difficult to square with James's habit of conducting prurient interrogations of newly-wed couples the morning after their wedding night. The facts may never be fully established and are anyway of less relevance to James's performance as a ruler than the sexual image he projected in public.

James's neglect of his image in fact stretched far beyond the sexual sphere and should probably be seen as his most serious fault. Elizabeth I had always fully appreciated the importance of image projection and had taken great care throughout her reign to display herself in the best possible light in order to retain her subjects' affections. James, however, did not accept that kingship was, as Conrad Russell (1992) has suggested, 'a thespian profession', and he therefore saw no need to continue her work. This might not have mattered quite so much had he not been so singularly lacking in personal dignity and charisma. While, as we have seen, some contemporary descriptions were guilty of exaggerating his distasteful mannerisms, James was certainly not an imposing man and he possessed little of the quality of 'majesty' which Elizabeth had placed at the core of the English monarchical style. This had not been a problem in Scotland for, as Jenny Wormald (1983) has shown, success there had depended upon much more informal personal interventions, and James had 'stepped down from his throne and joined in as one of the protagonists in the hurly-burly of debate'. It was, however, a serious drawback in England where the head of state was required to stand aloof and act as the chief player in a series of ritualized theatrical performances.

Although James cannot be blamed for his personality or for the fact that different styles of kingship operated in Edinburgh and London, he should perhaps be criticized for failing to make any attempt to fabricate an attractive image of his monarchy or to present himself as an admirable symbol to which his English subjects could relate. His failure in this area was noted by the ambassador from Venice who reported in 1607 that James did not 'caress the people, nor make them that good cheer the late Queen did, whereby she won their loves'. It was also noted by another contemporary commentator who remarked that:

> The access of the people made him so impatient that he often dispersed them with frowns, and on being told that they only wished to see his face, he cried out: 'God's wounds! I will pull down my breeches and they shall also see my arse.

One final aspect of James's personal make-up which also on occasion reduced his effectiveness as English king was his fragile health. When he succeeded Elizabeth in 1603 he was approaching middle age and, although his health held up through the early years of the reign, during the second half he was often incapacitated by illness. D. H. Willson (1956) is almost certainly mistaken in dating the beginning of a serious physical deterioration as early as 1616, but James was dangerously ill in 1619 and he may never have fully recovered thereafter. He suffered from frequent attacks of gout, arthritis, diarrhoea, and kidney pain, and he was periodically laid low by bouts of abdominal pain, nausea, and irregular breathing, which may have been caused by one of the porphyrias, a set of congenital diseases of the nervous system.

James Stuart the man was, therefore, far from ideally suited to performing the various roles and duties expected of him as English king. Furthermore, like all monarchs he made mistakes and misjudgements, and he laboured for much of his reign under the serious misapprehension that he could rule effectively on a semi-retired basis by employing the same tactics which had proved so successful in Scotland. It is important to remember, however, that by the early seventeenth century the 'job description' of the English head of state had become extremely daunting, and that James's relative unsuitability for the task was a quality he shared with the vast majority of his contemporaries; supreme practitioners of the art of kingship, like Elizabeth I, were very few and far between. How James coped in practice with the variety of problems he encountered as English king will be considered in the following sections.

2

The court, favourites, and patronage

By the early seventeenth century the principal royal courts of Europe had evolved into highly complex and sophisticated organisms, which played a major role in determining the political and cultural environments of the kingdoms within which they existed. As well as providing forums for the displaying of artistic and literary talent, they had become the central arenas within which powerful political factions fought each other for pre-eminence, and ambitious individuals vied for a share of the wealth and power dispensed through the patronage system. The key to success within the hierarchical and ritualized world of the court was the achieving and maintaining of personal access to the most powerful figures and ultimately to the monarch, the mainstay of the whole system. It was an important truism of early-modern society that rulers set the tone of their courts and that the behaviour of courtiers mirrored to a considerable degree the personal character and conduct of the presiding monarch. Historians have tended to confirm this view. They have suggested, for example, that the atmosphere of fear and suspicion which prevailed at Henry VIII's court was a product of Henry's own paranoid tendencies and that the moderation and formality of Elizabeth's court proceeded from the restraint of the queen's private life in her mature years. In the same way the Jacobean court, which has been roundly condemned as corrupt, drunken, promiscuous, and wasteful, has been seen as reflecting all the worst failings of James himself.

Sir Walter Ralegh's damning verdict on James's court was that it shone 'like rotten wood', and there is no doubt that it was notorious for its extravagance, venality, and moral laxity. While such phenomena were by no means new, the general standard of behaviour among courtiers does appear to have declined after 1603, and the relative frugality of Elizabeth's last years gave way to a round of lavish expenditure which persisted throughout the reign and remained impervious to a mounting chorus of disapproval and to the deepening crisis in crown finances. Colourful illustrations of the unrestrained and amoral nature of life at the Jacobean court are not difficult to find. The ultimate symbol of the apparently effortless extravagance was the ante-supper. This was introduced by one of the king's Scottish favourites, James Hay, earl of Carlisle, whose motto was 'Spend and God will send'. It involved the presentation to the assembled guests of a complete banquet, which was then promptly taken away and discarded before being replaced by a second set of dishes. When Hay decided to hold an ante-supper at court to celebrate Twelfth Night in 1621, 100 cooks spent twelve days preparing 1,600 dishes, and the total cost of the feast was around £3,300, a sum equivalent to the annual income of some of the more wealthy English landowners.

As well as being ruinously expensive, many Jacobean court festivities were also conspicuously lacking in modesty and refinement. A vivid picture of the riotous scenes which marked the visit to England in 1606 of James's brother-in-law, Christian IV of Denmark, was given by the courtier Sir John Harington. At one uninhibited banquet at Theobalds, the earl of Salisbury's house, the Danish king became so incapacitated by drink that he had to be put to bed, and some of the courtiers who were attempting to present a masque before the royal party were quite unable to perform and ended up 'sick and spewing in the lower hall'. Harington, who had spent a number of years observing both Elizabeth's and James's courts, summed up his disapproval by observing: 'I did never see such lack of good order, discretion, and sobriety as I have now done.' It could be argued that Harington was not an entirely unbiased observer and that these events were somewhat exceptional. It should also not be forgotten that James's court did have its more attractive

15

side; the court that invented the ante-supper was, for example, an extremely literary court which patronized major writers, such as John Donne, Ben Jonson, and William Shakespeare. None the less, most contemporaries and historians have agreed that there was a marked deterioration in standards at the English court after James's accession.

Such a decline would not have mattered so much if it had been visible only to those who lived or worked within the confines of the court. In the seventeenth century as now, however, the activities and behaviour of those most closely associated with the monarch were widely reported and discussed, and the latest news of James's court was disseminated throughout the country both in the private manuscript correspondence of individuals like Harington and in the growing numbers of early printed newsbooks. Descriptions of episodes like the drunken spree at Theobalds could have done little to commend James and his courtiers to the more sober members of the English political nation. Far more serious for the public image of the court and its king, however, was the reaction in the country to the scandalous relevations which surfaced in the middle years of the reign concerning the marriage of Frances Howard, countess of Essex, to James's favourite, Robert Carr, earl of Somerset, and the subsequent murder of Carr's follower, Sir Thomas Overbury.

This sordid episode – which possessed all the ingredients so beloved by the editors of the modern tabloid press – first came to the public's attention in 1613 when Frances Howard, who had become Carr's lover, initiated divorce proceedings against her husband, the earl of Essex, on the grounds of his sexual impotence. The accusation was subsequently investigated by a tribunal of clergymen which subjected Essex to considerable public embarrassment before succumbing to royal pressure and granting the divorce which left Howard free to marry Carr. Shortly afterwards, one of Carr's followers, Sir Thomas Overbury, who had opposed his marriage to Howard and may have been in possession of documents which could have proved damaging to his master and his new wife, suddenly died in the Tower of London. Some time later information came to light which implicated Frances Howard in Overbury's poisoning, and, after Sir Edward Coke had conducted a detailed investigation into the matter, she and Carr were arrested and subsequently put on trial for murder. Found guilty in 1616, their death sentences were waived by James and they were imprisoned for just six years.

As the details of this squalid affair spread throughout the country, growing numbers of James's subjects were forced to conclude that the court had become a thoroughly corrupt and wicked institution. As a consequence, in direct contrast to Elizabeth's reign when the court had been widely admired as the embodiment of all the nation's virtues, by the middle years of James's reign a damaging gap had been allowed to open up between the moral and cultural values of the court and those of the rest of the country. Lawrence Stone (1972) has argued that contemporaries perceived this gap in terms of a set of polarities. He has suggested that the political nation in the provinces viewed the court as 'wicked', 'extravagant', 'corrupt', 'promiscuous and homosexual', 'drunken', 'diseased', 'sycophantic', and 'popish', while regarding itself in contrast as 'virtuous', 'thrifty', 'honest', 'chaste and heterosexual', 'sober', 'healthy', 'outspoken', and 'solidly Protestant'. Historians have recently become wary about identifying opposing court and country factions within the sphere of Jacobean high politics. They should not, though, feel the same reluctance to acknowledge that, as a result of the debased image of the royal court, by 1625 a deep and damaging cultural fault-line separated James's royal palaces from the country seats of the English gentry and aristocracy.

As well as being censured for its general moral decline, the Jacobean court came under heavy criticism from contemporaries both inside and outside its walls for a number of other reasons; these included the dominance of James's Scottish entourage, the excessive reliance of the king upon his most prominent male favourites, and the abuse of the patronage system, particularly during the period of Buckingham's pre-eminence at the end of the reign.

When James came south from Edinburgh in 1603 he brought with him a number of his closest and most trusted friends, some of whom subsequently acquired prominent positions at his new court. Although they should not perhaps have expected anything else, many of the old queen's courtiers were extremely upset to discover that they were not, as Conrad Russell (1990) has put it, 'the only pebbles on the British beach', and they reacted to the newcomers with an overtly racist display of contempt and hostility. Despite James's genuine desire for greater mutual understanding, the Scots continued to act as a shield between James and his English courtiers, and the resultant animosity persisted throughout the reign. The predominant English view was nicely expressed by Sir John Holles who claimed in parliament in 1610 that: 'The Scottish monopolize his princely person, standing like mountains betwixt the beams of his grace and us.' The difficulties which James encountered in attempting to integrate his old and new courts stemmed not only from the personalities involved, but also from the divergent conventions that prevailed in Edinburgh and London. For while James's Scottish court had been an easy-going, informal place which, as Neil Cuddy (1987) has argued, allowed courtiers a 'relatively free and open access' to the king, the English court was much more rigidly layered and compartmentalized, and was deliberately designed for 'the preservation of distance' from the monarch.

The new Jacobean court was erected in May 1603 when the king reached Theobalds on his way south to London. In deciding on its personnel, James adopted the principle of 'equal partition', by which positions were to be divided up equally between the Scots and the English. The area of the court where this new approach was most fully put into practice was the privy chamber, where the forty-eight posts were distributed half to the English and half to the Scots. The gentlemen of the privy chamber were in regular contact with the sovereign, attending on him when he gave formal audiences and eating with him when he dined in public. They did not, however, enjoy anything like the same degree of easy access to James as those who were appointed to the closest circle around the king, the bedchamber. Had the king applied the equal partition policy here too, he might well have avoided many of the unpleasant ethnic quarrels which were to dog life at court throughout the reign. But when it came to choosing his most intimate friends and confidants, James was not prepared to surround himself with strangers, and all sixteen posts in the new bedchamber were given to members of his Scottish entourage.

This Scottish monopoly of the bedchamber, which Cuddy (1987) has labelled 'the most important substantive product of the political settlement of the succession', persisted until the last

18

years of the reign. Only one Englishman, Sir Philip Herbert, was appointed to the bedchamber before 1615; if his elevation, along with that of the Scot, Sir James Hay, in 1605 was meant as the first step in the extension of the equal partition principle to this inner ring of the court, the idea was subsequently abandoned, perhaps as a result of the final dashing of James's hopes for a union of his two kingdoms in 1607. It was only after the rise of Buckingham that the English began to break through into the bedchamber in significant numbers. Buckingham himself was appointed in 1615, and by 1622 eight bedchamber posts – nearly half the total – were occupied by Englishmen.

James's main reason for excluding his new subjects from the bedchamber for so long was his intense concern for his own safety, for he seems to have felt secure only when surrounded by his oldest and most trusted friends. While the monarch was always, of course, exposed to some degree of danger, men like Sir Thomas Erskine, later earl of Kellie, who personally controlled all access to the king for much of the reign, had a very strong vested interest in encouraging James in the fears and suspicions which made him so dependent on them. If the Scots were the beneficiaries of James's insecurity, the losers were the increasingly resentful and xenophobic English courtiers and politicians who struggled in vain to breach the impenetrable protective ring around James. Although the point is disputed by Pauline Croft (1991), Neil Cuddy (1987) has suggested that even as powerful a figure as Robert Cecil, earl of Salisbury, who had helped James to secure the succession to the English throne during Elizabeth's last years and was in overall charge of the government from 1603 until his death in 1612, was prevented by the bedchamber from seeing the king as often as he wished. James's refusal to open up the bedchamber to his new subjects was the cause of a great deal of discontent and division and an important factor behind the fierce opposition in his first parliament to the idea of a union of his two kingdoms. It is tempting, therefore, to criticize James for a serious and avoidable misjudgement arising out of an irrational paranoia. Conrad Russell (1992), however, has recently come to his defence over this issue, arguing that, as an absentee king of Scotland, James was entirely justified in retaining a Scottish bedchamber as an essential means of keeping in touch with political developments in his northern kingdom.

James has also received much contemporary and historical criticism for his extreme reliance on, and generosity to, his male favourites. While most contemporaries were willing to accept that monarchs needed their playthings, James's relationships were disapproved of both because his favourites were men and also because he allowed them to interfere in important political matters. In England, James's two principal favourites were Robert Carr, earl of Somerset, who held a pre-eminent position in the king's affections from 1607 until the Overbury murder trial in 1615, and George Villiers, duke of Buckingham, who took Carr's place and retained an extraordinary hold over James until 1625.

Robert Carr began his career as a page in Scotland and travelled south with James in 1603 as a member of Sir James Hay's retinue. He came to James's attention four years later after falling from his horse while jousting. James decided to take personal responsibility for nursing the attractive young man back to health, and before long he was telling his councillors that he did 'more delight in his company and conversation than in any man's living'. Over the next few years Carr was showered with money, gifts, and lands, including the manor of Sherborne in Dorset which the king had seized from Sir Walter Ralegh's trustees. In 1611 he was raised to the peerage as viscount Rochester and in 1613 created earl of Somerset. Carr began to dabble in politics in 1610 when he expressed his opposition to the Great Contract which was then under discussion in parliament. He became more fully involved in 1612, when the death of Salisbury ushered in a period of intense factional conflict at court. While he himself lacked the necessary intelligence and guile to succeed in an area where good looks were no guarantee of success, he was for a while ably guided through the murky waters of Jacobean politics by his unscrupulous follower, Sir Thomas Overbury. Overbury was implacably opposed to the powerful Howard faction, and it was in order to detach Carr from his influence and to re-align him with their camp that the Howards later tempted Carr with the bait of a marriage to his lover, Frances Howard. When Overbury tried to obstruct this match, he was, as we have seen, disposed of with consequences which were ultimately fatal for both Carr and the Howards.

The vacuum at court created by Carr's disgrace was quickly filled by another handsome young man, George Villiers, who was destined to rise to even greater heights than his predecessor, but also to become infinitely more unpopular. Although cleverer than Carr, Villiers owed his prominence entirely to his beauty and charm, which he used to captivate not only James but the queen, Prince Charles, and many other men and women at court too. A number of contemporary descriptions testified to his great physical attractions, and in particular to his delicate facial features and long, slender arms and legs. Bishop Goodman observed that: 'there was no blemish in him', and the earl of Clarendon was also struck by the 'beauty and gracefulness of his person'; even the hostile puritan Sir Simonds D'Ewes was forced to admit that he was attractive, although he added: 'his hands and face seemed to me especially effeminate'. A good impression of his striking physical appearance can still be gained from the anonymous full-length portrait in the National Portrait Gallery in London.

It was precisely because of his looks that Villiers was deliberately brought to James's attention in 1614 by the enemies of the Howards in the hope that he might displace Carr in the king's heart. The ploy was if anything too successful. James soon fell deeply in love with Villiers, and over the next few years he heaped honours on the young man he nicknamed 'Steenie' because, like St Stephen, he looked like an angel. In April 1615 Villiers became only the second Englishman to be appointed to the bedchamber. In January 1616 he became master of the king's horse, and a mere twelve months later he was created earl of Buckingham. By the end of 1618 he had effectively destroyed the power of his enemies, the Howards, and achieved a dominance at court which he was to retain throughout the remainder of James's reign and on into Charles's. James allowed him to amass so much wealth and power primarily because he was besotted with him, but also because Buckingham was an able and energetic administrator who kept his promises to the king and dealt effectively with the constant stream of requests for favour and advancement that James found so tiresome. By the early 1620s those responsible for introducing Villiers to James had seen their pawn go on to capture a king and control the whole chessboard.

Few men in English history can have been viewed with quite the same degree of public fear and detestation as Buckingham was during the 1620s. There were a number of distinct reasons for this intense unpopularity. Within the confines of the court Buckingham met with some snobbish resentment because of what were seen as his low social origins as a member of an ancient but relatively obscure landed family from Leicestershire. He was also criticized for missing no opportunity to distribute money and honours to his family; by 1625 both his brothers had been raised to the peerage and a whole tribe of more distant relatives had received titles, gifts, or pensions. It had also become very difficult for aspiring courtiers and civil servants to gain advancement without marrying into the Villiers clan.

It was, however, the fact that by the early 1620s Buckingham had acquired an unprecedented control over patronage that caused the most resentment among courtiers. Linda Levy Peck (1986) has suggested that he was responsible for introducing several unfortunate distortions into the operation of a patronage system which was already under great structural pressure as a result of increasing demand and diminishing resources. Well aware that he had risen from nowhere and lacked any significant power base outside the court, Buckingham knew he could survive only by destroying all rival sources of patronage. He therefore insisted both that his clients should have no other patrons and that nobody should be seen to achieve advancement without at least his formal blessing. When, for example, Sir Henry Yelverton was preferred for the post of attorney-general in 1617 over Buckingham's own nominee, the favourite insisted that Yelverton should allow him to take the warrant of appointment to James for approval. Buckingham was also heavily criticized for seeing grants of honours as purely business transactions, and for divesting them of any sense of being merited rewards for honourable royal service; during parliament's attempt to impeach him in 1626 one speaker argued that he had turned the royal bounty into a merchant's contract. There is no doubt that those who received honours during Buckingham's period of ascendancy were generally less deserving than those elevated before 1616. Furthermore, as Kevin Sharpe (1986) has pointed out, many of them were conspicuously lacking in local connections, a fact which did nothing to ease the troubled relations between the court and the provinces.

As far as a wider public opinion was concerned, Buckingham was despised by English men and women of all social classes for his enthralment of James, for his family's links with popery, and for his alleged dabbling in witchcraft and the black arts. During the early 1620s his interference in important issues of foreign policy, and in particular his involvement in Prince Charles's journey to Madrid in 1623, only further increased his unpopularity with the political nation. In his biography of the duke, Roger Lockyer (1981) has attempted to rescue Buckingham from earlier accusations of extreme political incompetence. He has argued that his reading of the international scene during the early part of the Thirty Years War was essentially sound and that English foreign policy was unsuccessful primarily because of a lack of money to pursue it with sufficient vigour. He has, however, been too generous to his subject; Buckingham's headlong dash for war after his return from Madrid was impetuous and ill-judged, and, as Simon Adams (1983) has shown, he was mistaken in believing that the French could be persuaded to join a general anti-Habsburg alliance in 1624.

James's relationship with Buckingham clearly, therefore, did him no credit in the eyes of the majority of his subjects. It should, however, be remembered that, while James was prepared to stand by and allow the duke to destroy his rivals as court patrons, he did not permit him to silence those in the government who held alternative political opinions. Even when Buckingham was at the very height of his power, James continued to listen to his other privy councillors and received from them a range of conflicting advice on important issues such as the proposed Spanish Match. Nor did the king ever relinquish his own firm control over religious and foreign policy. When Buckingham tried to pressurize James into going to war in 1624, he succeeded only in threatening his own unique place in the king's affections. Indeed, following James's death in 1625 it was very widely asserted and believed that he had poisoned the king in order to prevent his own fall from power. Although Buckingham had undoubtedly acquired immense power by 1625, he was given a great deal more by Charles, and any damage he inflicted upon the Stuart monarchy during James's last years pales into relative insignificance when compared with the disasters he presided over between 1625 and 1628.

3

Financial problems

James inherited from Elizabeth I both a substantial debt of around £420,000 and a crown suffering from the effects of serious long-term under-funding. As the debt was substantially more than the queen's average annual income at the end of her reign, it could in no way be considered inconsequential; equally, though, it should not be seen as a crushing millstone around the new king's neck or as the prime cause of his later financial difficulties. Indeed, if one takes into account the fact that £300,000 of the sum parliament had voted Elizabeth in 1601 had still not been received by the Exchequer at the time of her death, and that another £100,000 of the money owed had been collected in the late 1590s as forced loans which nobody realistically expected the crown to repay, it could be argued that Elizabeth had died solvent. But if the debt was manageable, the under-funding was much more intractable. Over the course of the Tudor period, the disposable income of the English monarchy had dramatically decreased in real terms. This had happened partly because the prolonged price inflation of the sixteenth century had eroded the purchasing power of an income which had proved difficult to 'index-link', and partly because the English tax-paying classes had manoeuvred themselves into the enviable position where they gave only sporadic and relatively meagre financial support to a monarchy which was expected to meet all its own peacetime expenses.

The English crown received its income from several distinct sources. As a very large landowner in its own right, it enjoyed a substantial rental income and was also able to sell off portions of its land to realize quick cash. Although such alienation of property gradually reduced the total revenue from rents and had an adverse effect on the crown's status and image, Elizabeth had raised money in this way at regular intervals throughout her reign and James was obliged to continue the process. The English monarch also received revenue from customs levies and from a number of feudal dues, the most important of which was wardship. The right to collect customs duties – or 'tonnage and poundage' – on selected exports and imports was a traditional royal privilege, which was normally renewed at the beginning of each reign. The levels of duty were set down in a Book of Rates which was periodically revised. During Mary Tudor's reign the crown had managed to extend its customs rights by charging new 'impositions' on previously exempt goods. This innovation was retained by Elizabeth and was to be greatly expanded under James. The sums raised through customs and impositions were significant and growing; in the late 1580s they had accounted for about one third of total crown revenue, and by 1611 this proportion had risen to one half.

Wardship, a legacy of an earlier medieval age, was another important source of revenue for the crown, but one which caused great annoyance to English landed society in the century preceding the civil war. When a landowner who held a feudal tenure from the crown died leaving a minor as his heir, the young person along with all the family estates fell under the control of the crown. The original idea behind the practice had been that the sovereign would thus be better able to protect the minor from rapacious neighbours, but ironically by the early seventeenth century the head of state had become the chief accomplice of those seeking to exploit the situation. Wardships were by now systematically sold off by the crown to speculators who paid large sums to the Court of Wards and who subsequently recouped their cash and made substantial additional profits through the ruthless exploitation of their wards' estates. To add insult to injury, when a ward finally came of age he was forced to pay a cash sum to the crown for the right to take possession of his often devastated property.

The other significant element in royal income was parliamentary taxation. By 1600 the principal tax was the subsidy, which, along with the levies of fifteenths and tenths which often accompanied it, was collected by the crown following specific one-off grants by individual parliaments. As a revenue source it had several serious drawbacks. Since it was by its very nature an occasional tax, it could in no way be depended upon, and parliaments usually expected some concessions in return for granting it. In addition, by the early seventeenth century the yield from the subsidy had seriously declined from its mid-Tudor level. Whereas Elizabeth I had received about £137,000 for a single subsidy at the beginning of her reign, the combined effect of tax evasion and corruption and inefficiency in the assessment arrangements had reduced this to only £72,500 by 1621. When allowance is also made for the inflation that had occurred during these years, the real value of the 1621 subsidy becomes only about one fifth of that of the 1559 grant.

By the beginning of James's reign probably no more than 10 per cent of households in the country were still officially required to pay the subsidy, and even this small proportion was escaping very lightly by modern standards. Several years before James's accession Sir Walter Ralegh had commented that 'our estates that be £30 or £40 in the Queen's [subsidy] books are not the hundredth part of our wealth', and throughout the early seventeenth century the country's richest landowners, who were worth thousands of pounds annually, were required to pay only a couple of hundred pounds when a subsidy was granted. The great majority of tax-payers were, of course, more than happy with this state of affairs and particularly anxious that their representatives in parliament should do nothing to alter it. What was appreciated by only a very small group of them was that, had they been prepared to raise significantly the level of supply they gave to the crown, they might have won a corresponding increase in the bargaining power wielded by parliament. As it was, while the impoverished crown could ill afford to forgo any sources of revenue, the sums on offer from parliament were never sufficient to provide an effective remedy for what James called 'the eating canker of want'.

It was, therefore, particularly unfortunate that in 1603 a public revenue system which, in Conrad Russell's (1990) phrase, was already 'close to the point of breakdown' was inherited by a man who was quite incapable of adhering to the tight budgetary constraints so vital to financial well-being. At the start of the reign, James's advisers lost no time in correcting his mistaken impression that the English crown was rich, and soon made him aware of the real difficulty of his financial situation. Over the next few years James frequently expressed a willingness to co-operate with them in their attempts to improve the situation; in 1607, for example, he promised the privy council that he was willing to adopt 'such remedies and antidotes as ye shall apply unto my disease'. None the less, for the deep-rooted psychological reasons discussed above, he proved unable either to deny himself expensive pleasures or to restrain himself from dispensing gifts on a grand scale to those around him. As Bishop Hacket later concluded: 'for thrift and saving he could never be brought to think of them'. The result was that after 1603 royal spending rose dramatically. In comparison to the £300,000 annual expenditure incurred by Elizabeth during the last years of her reign when the country was at war, James was soon spending £400,000 a year in peacetime, and by 1614 his outgoings had climbed to £550,000.

Some of this increase was inevitable and fully anticipated by English observers. James clearly needed to spend some money to equip his court and to buy support from his new subjects; he also incurred the unavoidable early expenses of the old queen's funeral, his own official entry into London, and his coronation. Similarly, he was obliged to spend some money to compensate for Elizabeth's extreme meanness during her last years, a policy which had built up considerable pressure for rewards and preferment and had offended against the widely accepted principle that 'for a king not to be bountiful were a fault'. Furthermore, unlike Elizabeth, James had a family, which involved him in both regular ongoing expenditure and occasional extraordinary payments. Both his wife and eldest son needed their own households, and the cost of Prince Henry's alone rose from £3,660 in 1604–5 to £35,765 in 1610–11. The one-off family expenses included the enormous sum of £116,000 that James had to find during 1612 and 1613 for the funeral of his son Henry and the wedding of his daughter Elizabeth.

None the less, the scale of the rise in expenditure far exceeded anything that could be justified by these factors. From the start of the reign, huge sums were spent on fees and pensions, generous gifts, and lavish court entertainments. Between 1603 and 1607, for example, the king gave away gifts to the value of £68,000 and pensions worth £30,000, and by 1610 the annual expenditure on fees and annuities had increased to £80,000, as compared with the £30,000 spent annually by Elizabeth. The earl of Clarendon later claimed that James had bestowed on one favourite, James Hay, earl of Carlisle, a total of £400,000 – a sum equivalent to one year's entire crown revenue. During the first five years of the reign the average annual costs of the Wardrobe increased to £36,500, a massive jump from the average of £9,500 spent during the last four years of Elizabeth's reign. Similarly, the annual cost of running the Household, which was responsible for providing the court's food and looking after the royal stables, rose from £64,000 during Elizabeth's last year to over £100,000 by 1611. During the first nine years of his reign James also spent a total of £185,000 on jewels. The inevitable result of all this self-indulgence and largess was a steady growth in the royal debt. By 1606 this had doubled to £816,000, and, while it was reduced over the next few years to £300,000 as a result of the efforts of Robert Cecil, by 1613 it was up again to £500,000, and in 1618 it reached £900,000 – double the amount James was receiving as his annual income. For all his subsequent hard work, Lionel Cranfield only managed to reduce it slightly by 1625.

The unenviable job of keeping the royal finances afloat in this sea of conspicuous consumption fell to James's principal financial ministers. Their struggle either to rein in the spiralling costs or to increase revenues in line with them persisted throughout the reign. The first man to come to grips with the financial imbroglio was Robert Cecil, earl of Salisbury. As chief secretary of state, Cecil worked closely with James's first lord treasurer, Thomas Sackville, earl of Dorset, during the early years of the reign, and after Sackville's death in 1608 he succeeded him at the treasury. Cecil employed several new tactics in the hope of restricting James's scope for liberality. In 1608 he persuaded him to accept a 'Book of Bounty', which set down agreed levels for crown gifts and pensions. The following year he persuaded James to accept a plan which restricted his freedom to sell off his lands for cash; the most valuable crown estates were placed in entail, a legal device which stipulated that they must be retained and handed down to James's heirs after his death.

Aware, however, that maintaining tight control over James's

spending was extraordinarily difficult, Cecil concentrated most of his effort on increasing income. In 1604 he issued a new Book of Rates for the customs, to replace the one that had been used since the 1550s, and shortly afterwards he decided to farm out – or privatize – the customs by allowing a business consortium to collect the duties in exchange for a payment of £112,400 a year. This figure was subsequently increased to £120,000 in 1607, £136,000 in 1611, and £140,000 in 1614, sums which represented a marked increase over the £100,000 received annually at the end of Elizabeth's reign. More significantly, after the crown had confirmed the legality of impositions by successfully suing the merchant John Bate for non-payment in 1606, Cecil seized the opportunity to issue a further Book of Rates in 1608 and to extend the tariffs to cover a much wider range of imported goods. These new impositions immediately brought an additional £70,000 a year to the crown, and over the course of the next twenty-five years their yield increased steadily to more than £200,000 a year.

Cecil also achieved increases in the revenue received from crown lands and wardship. After undertaking a great deal of time-consuming and painstaking research into the records of the crown estates, he managed to obtain an extra £100,000 from rental income and to recover £200,000 in the form of outstanding debts. Similarly, by insisting that the Court of Wards adopt a more hard-headed entrepreneurial approach, he raised its profits from £14,000 in 1603 to £23,000 in 1612. The cumulative effect of all this work was to increase the total royal income from £315,000 in 1606 to around £460,000 by 1610, and to reduce the royal debt by about half a million pounds. This was an impressive achievement, but one that failed to outlive its creator, for after 1612 all the progress that Cecil had made towards solvency was wiped out by the continuing inexorable rise in spending.

In an attempt to transcend these short-term expedients and to restructure public revenue in a way which would create an altogether more stable financial base for James, Cecil devised in 1610 the plan which became known as the Great Contract. He suggested that in return for an annual grant of £200,000 from parliament, the king should surrender his feudal rights of wardship and purveyance (which empowered him to purchase goods and services for the royal Household at below market rates). After long and intense discussion, both James and parliament rejected the deal, the king because he decided that to sell the 'flower of his regality' for cash would be a form of prostitution, and the MPs because they baulked at the size of the sum involved and objected to the principle of regular taxation. Whether the adoption of the Great Contract would have provided a solution to the financial problems which continued to sour relations between the Stuarts and their subjects up to 1642 must remain a matter for speculation.

During the six years following Cecil's death in 1612, James entrusted the management of his finances first to a group of commissioners and then to a far less capable and conscientious treasurer, Thomas Howard, earl of Suffolk. The initiatives that occurred during this period were aimed almost entirely at increasing revenue. Suffolk collected £65,000 from the country in 1614 as a free gift or 'benevolence', and another £200,000 was subsequently received from the Dutch in exchange for the withdrawal of English garrisons from the United Provinces. It was also during these years that the device of selling off titles for cash started to be exploited to the full. The practice had begun early in the reign with the sale of knighthoods and was extended in 1611 with the creation of the baronetcy. This new title, which could be purchased for £1,095 by anyone owning land worth £1,000 or more a year, had raised £90,000 for the crown by 1614. In 1615 the crown also put full peerages up for sale at £10,000 each, with the result that over the next ten years the number of English earls more than doubled. Lawrence Stone (1965) has estimated that between 1603 and 1629 the crown benefited by at least £620,000 from the sale of honours, but this apparently painless revenue source did have some serious repercussions as it brought the crown into disrespect and created some considerable animosity between the old and the new peers.

Suffolk also had high hopes of two other possible revenue sources: the Spanish marriage and the Cokayne Project. Both had the potential to provide a remedy for the financial difficulties, but neither proved a success.

Following the beginning of negotiations for a marriage between Prince Charles and the Spanish infanta in 1614, Suffolk and the other members of the pro-Spanish Howard faction at court pressed hard for the match, seeing a Spanish dowry of around £600,000 as the windfall that would release the government from its dire financial predicament. Cranfield too was initially hopeful, and it was only after Charles's disastrous trip to Madrid in 1623 that the dowry was finally eliminated from financial calculations.

In 1614 a London merchant, William Cokayne, persuaded the government to suspend the charter of the Merchant Adventurers Company, prohibit the export of unfinished cloth, and hand over to him the sole right to export finished or dressed cloth. In exchange, he guaranteed the government a large increase in the customs revenue that would accrue from the export of the more valuable finished cloth; in the event, however, the scheme precipitated a major crisis in the cloth industry and caused a significant fall in customs receipts.

The astute and capable businessman, Lionel Cranfield, began to make a name for himself as a financial reformer in 1618 through his work as a treasury commissioner and master of the Wardrobe and Court of Wards, and three years later he succeeded the ineffectual Henry Montague, viscount Mandeville, as lord treasurer. Like Cecil, he attempted a two-pronged approach to financial reform, but, while he achieved some useful increases in revenue by uncovering concealed crown lands and forcing up the rent paid by the customs farmers, it is for his labours to reduce the costs of James's government and Household that he is chiefly remembered.

In order to cut down on crown pensions, which by now used up about one sixth of James's income, he re-issued Cecil's Book of Bounty in 1619, and two years later he demanded that James place an immediate moratorium on the payment of all pensions. He also made substantial reductions in the large Household budget by implementing a range of minor economies, such as reducing the number of courses served at dinner, and he made strenuous efforts to eradicate a range of wasteful practices from government departments. As a result of his constant hard work and vigilance, in 1620 Cranfield achieved a goal that had eluded all his predecessors by balancing James's books and bringing ordinary expenditure into line with income. He could not, however, find a way to prevent the court undermining this achievement by squandering large amounts on special projects, like Charles's trip to Madrid in 1623 which cost £120,000. Nor did he manage to make any substantial reduction in the royal debt. Furthermore, his cost-cutting activities made him highly unpopular, especially among those whose power depended upon their ability to dispense patronage. By 1624 he had fallen foul of the duke of Buckingham, who removed him from the scene by secretly encouraging parliament to impeach him.

While James's treasury ministers managed to keep the crown's financial head just above water until 1625, fundamental and lasting reform proved an unattainable goal. To some extent this was because it would have required a frontal assault on the endemic corruption and the vested interest of all those with a stake in the system. That Suffolk's prime achievement as treasurer was the erection of a sumptuous palace for himself at Audley End is well known, but even the most committed reformers, like Cecil and Cranfield, made sure that their own nests were handsomely feathered. Significant long-term improvement was also ruled out by James's incurable extravagance and the refusal of the political nation to concede the need to grant him a regular and adequate financial supply. For all his good intentions and the constant nagging of his ministers, James was never able to change his prodigal ways. Deep down he continued to resent those like Cranfield who tried to curb his extravagance, suspecting, as Bishop Hacket put it, that 'they loved him not'. Similarly, all attempts to increase taxation to a more realistic level were successfully resisted, and three years after James's death one of his son's councillors could still claim in exasperation that the French king received more in taxes from the duchy of Normandy alone than the English king did from his entire realm.

The key point is that these last two obstacles were inextricably linked. The worst aspect of James's extravagance was not that it wasted large quantities of cash which could and should have been employed for more useful ends, but rather that it made it much harder for the majority of MPs to appreciate that there was an underlying structural problem with the public finances, and that it gave the small minority, who might privately have acknowledged that there was such a defect, the perfect excuse not to take the necessary, but unpopular, corrective action. Like someone who has given money to an impoverished friend only to find him or her in a public house a few minutes later buying drinks for a large crowd, James's MPs became increasingly sceptical about his claims of poverty and determined not to consider any course of action which might enable him to squander even greater sums. As a consequence, while Cecil and Cranfield ensured that James avoided financial ruin, neither man was able to make the changes that would have restored the monarchy to permanent financial health. Nor were they able to gather together the resources which would have allowed their master to fight a major war with any real prospect of success. As James assiduously avoided resorting to this course of action, this did not matter very much before 1625; but when war with Spain did arrive shortly after Charles's accession, it was to prove financially calamitous.

4

James I and his parliaments

In the old Whig historical tradition, the accession of James I in 1603 was seen as an important watershed in English parliamentary history, marking the beginning of serious constitutional conflict between crown and parliament. According to Whig historians, whereas Elizabeth had been committed to her parliaments and had generally managed to achieve productive working accommodations with them, James found his parliaments incomprehensible and annoying and soon resolved to dispense with them altogether. By deliberately setting out in this way to destroy the native parliamentary liberties of the English people, he provoked a determined opposition movement within parliament, which, in the course of the ensuing struggles with the crown, ultimately gained the necessary organization and confidence to resist the Stuarts with military force. James was thus responsible for launching the country on to a 'high road to civil war', a route his son proceeded along with equal determination after 1625. This analysis, which enjoyed its heyday during the Victorian period through the work of influential historians such as Macaulay and Gardiner, was carried into the twentieth century by Trevelyan, and was still being confidently expounded as recently as the early 1970s by Wallace Notestein in *The House of Commons 1604–1610* (1971).

Since then the two central tenets of the classic Whig perspective – the emergence after 1603 of a parliamentary opposition which engaged in a fight to the death with an aggressive divine-right monarchy, and the status of James and Charles as the undisputed villains of the piece – have been called into question by a number of historians. In 1973 Alan G. R. Smith published an updated version of the Whig thesis which, while it did not dispute the existence of discord or of a well-organized parliamentary opposition, did question whether James should bear the primary blame for the appearance of these phenomena. Smith conceded that James had 'contributed substantially' to the creation of conflict by antagonizing his MPs with a number of highly unpopular policies, such as his proposed union with Scotland, his relaxed approach to Catholic recusancy, and his negotiations for a marriage alliance with Spain. Smith also accused James of neglecting to take the necessary steps to ensure the effective management of his parliaments, and in particular of failing to use his influential privy councillors and speakers as government spokesmen in the House of Commons. He pointed out, however, that as the membership of the Commons grew in numbers, intelligence, and political maturity during the late sixteenth and early seventeenth centuries, the MPs also became more organized and increasingly obsessed with defending their parliamentary privileges. For Smith the provocative stance adopted by MPs during the 1620s over such incidents as the Protestation, the condemnation of patents and monopolies, and the impeachment of Bacon and Cranfield was clear evidence of their determination to flex their newly-developed political muscle. He concluded that the conflicts between the king and his MPs were principally caused not by any failings on James's part but by the emergence of a 'new spirit' in parliament.

Several years after the appearance of Smith's article, Conrad Russell initiated a far more radical re-appraisal of Jacobean parliamentary history. In his seminal 'revisionist' article 'Parliamentary History in Perspective 1604–1629', published in 1976, he mounted a full-scale assault on the most basic canons of the Whig creed, arguing that parliaments in early-Stuart England were weak and declining and that they contained no oppositions in any meaningful sense of the word. As evidence of their powerlessness he cited their failure to use the threat of with-holding supply as a bargaining ploy against James, and their consequent inability to achieve one single objective against which the king had set his face. For Russell, incidents such as the impeachments of the early 1620s were evidence not that the MPs had become dynamic and aggressive opponents of royal government, but rather that they were the ready dupes of factions within the court. Dismissing talk of oppositions and deep ideological divides, he argued that James's backbench MPs shared with his privy councillors the same basic outlook on the important constitutional issues of the day, that many of them aspired to government posts, and that none of them held views 'incompatible with office'.

Over the following decade Russell (1979 and 1983) further developed this revisionist perspective, arguing that parliaments were entirely superfluous to the normal functioning of the state, and that the vast majority of MPs were much more interested in their own local issues than in national politics and had no desire to change this situation. He went so far as to claim that under James and Charles parliament was not an institution but a series of events and that its meetings should be viewed not as 'major historical events', but rather as *ad hoc* gatherings of men reacting to events taking place elsewhere'. This persuasive thesis began to win wide support from other historians, notably Kevin Sharpe (1978 and 1985), whose work confirmed the absence of ideological polarization and stressed the relative marginality of parliament when compared to the real seat of political power: the court.

For some years the revisionists carried all before them, but during the late 1980s what some have called a post-revisionist viewpoint began to emerge in the work of historians such as Richard Cust (1989a and 1989b), Ann Hughes (1991), and Thomas Cogswell (1989a and 1989b). While disclaiming any intention of rebuilding the old Whig edifice, these historians have suggested that, along with the Whig bath water, the revisionists had thrown out the baby of genuine ideological conflict. They have argued that there were real and important political issues which divided the government from the nation, that awareness of these issues was very widely disseminated both throughout the country and across the social spectrum, and that most MPs saw themselves as accountable to the political pressures applied by their constituents. They have also disputed Russell's contention that James's MPs failed to use the subsidy as a weapon, arguing instead that they frequently drove hard bargains and only granted money without strings once, in 1621. Thus, in direct contrast to the revisionists who had narrowed down the confines of Jacobean politics to the small world of the court and council chamber, these post-revisionist historians have once again widened the stage and cast-list of early-Stuart political history to embrace both Westminster and an interested and well-informed populace in the provinces.

Charting a safe course through this historiographical mine-field is no easy task, but some aspects of James's relationship with his parliaments are now relatively uncontentious. It is clear that James had little practical, day-to-day need for parliaments and that his government could function quite happily without them. Parliament was in session for a total of only thirty-six months during the course of James's twenty-two-year reign, and the only major legislative project which the king brought before his MPs was his proposal in 1604 for the union of England and Scotland. It may have been their early and – to James – entirely unreasonable negativity over this scheme that soured the king's relationship with them almost from the outset. Certainly James later made no secret of his annoyance with his English MPs. In 1610 he referred to them as 'this rotten seed of Egypt', and four years later, after the débâcle of the Addled Parliament, he fulminated against them to the Spanish ambassador, declaring:

> The House of Commons is a body without a head. The members give their opinions in a disorderly manner. At their meetings nothing is heard but cries, shouts, and confusion. I am surprised that my ancestors should ever have permitted it to come into existence. I am a stranger, and found it here when I arrived, so that I am obliged to put up with what I cannot get rid of.

This famous outburst has often been cited as proof of James's failure to understand the traditions of the English parliament and of his consequent over-sensitivity to the robust criticisms of his MPs. It might equally, however, be seen as evidence of the harmful consequences of a lack of parliamentary management since 1604. Jenny Wormald (1983), meanwhile, has suggested that James's disillusionment with the Westminster parliament may have been the result not of his lack of experience of such assemblies, but, on the contrary, of his prior knowledge of its counterpart in Edinburgh, which was in many ways a much more efficient institution.

The early days of James's first parliament in 1604 were dominated by a tussle over parliamentary privilege. When the Commons discovered that the government had sought to reverse the defeat suffered in the Buckinghamshire election by the privy councillor Sir John Fortescue, they responded by declaring that they alone had the right to resolve election disputes. This in turn provoked an angry reaction from James. According to the older tradition, this was the real beginning of the estrangement between king and parliament, but the revisionist R. C. Munden (1978a) has shown that James in fact handled the crisis well by suggesting the compromise of a new election, and that no permanent damage was caused by the row. Munden (1978b) has further suggested that Fortescue's election defeat should be attributed not to any anti-court sentiment on the part of independent Buckinghamshire freeholders, but to in-fighting within a privy council made insecure by the change in regime. The vexed questions of wardship and purveyance also surfaced early on in this parliament, but, although James showed some willingness to find a way to address these grievances, nothing was actually achieved.

The other issue that dominated parliamentary business up until 1607 was the plan to unite the two kingdoms of England and Scotland. In 1604 James was hoping that he could secure agreement on three points: the acceptance of the idea in principle, the adoption of the name 'Great Britain', and the appointment of commissioners to consider the detailed ramifications of the proposal. But while he was looking for an initial display of goodwill, he met instead implacable resistance and hostility, and was deeply shocked to discover that many of the MPs thoroughly detested and despised his compatriots. In the face of strong, racist opposition, James tried to save his scheme through compromise; when, for example, the judges decided that a change in the country's name would invalidate all existing English law, he promptly shelved this aspect of the scheme. This, however, did little to soften attitudes in the Commons, and by the summer of 1604 James was extremely angry and disappointed, while some of the MPs had decided to defend themselves in their famous 'Apology and Satisfaction'. Thereafter, the scheme encountered constant delays, and it was effectively abandoned in 1607 with parliament having made only relatively minor concessions to James, including an agreement that all those born in either kingdom after 1603 should ✗ hold dual nationality.

Although he might perhaps have taken greater care to explain to the Commons the detailed thinking behind the union project, James should not bear the bulk of the blame for its rejection or for the subsequent coolness in relations between himself and his English MPs. He had been careful to consult parliament throughout, and had always accepted that England would remain the dominant partner in any union. The scheme had been wrecked largely by the xenophobia of the English MPs and, according to the revisionists, of the English privy councillors too. Munden (1978a) has suggested that Cecil and his colleagues were among the fiercest opponents of the move and that, in order to avoid incurring the king's displeasure themselves, they used a gullible House of Commons to do their dirty work for them. Given his deep personal investment in a project that had much to commend it, James should perhaps be forgiven for feeling alienated from his new subjects as a result of their rebuff.

After further wrangles over impositions and the Great Contract, James dissolved his first parliament in 1610 on anything but amicable terms with its members, complaining that: 'these seven years last past . . . our fame and actions have been daily tossed like tennis balls amongst them, and all that spite and malice might do to disgrace and inflame us hath been used'.

James's next parliament met in 1614; as it proved almost entirely unproductive and failed to pass any legislation, it became known as the Addled Parliament. The king issued the writs for elections in the hope that the MPs would provide some money to ease his acute financial difficulties, but the session got off to a bad start when false rumours were spread suggesting that a group of 'undertakers' had agreed to manage the election for the king in order to produce an amenable house. When the Commons subsequently turned to the question of financial supply, they suggested that, in return for the grant of two subsidies, James should give up his right to collect impositions. As they were offering James a one-off payment of £140,000 and asking him to forgo an annual income of £70,000, this was a deal that James could in no way afford to accept, and he dissolved parliament in June without a grant of subsidy. A number of historians have attributed the failure of the Addled Parliament to the in-fighting of the various factions within the king's privy council. They have argued that, having failed in its attempt to prevent the parliament meeting, the powerful Howard group, led by the earls of Northampton, Suffolk, and Somerset, worked behind the scenes to sour relations between the government and the MPs, with the aim of discrediting their rival, the earl of Pembroke, who had been the chief supporter of the decision to summon the assembly. Linda Levy Peck (1981 and 1982) has attempted to defend the earl of Northampton against such charges, claiming that he was not primarily motivated by a desire to wreck the parliament and was prepared to be conciliatory towards the MPs on occasions. Her rigorous defence of the earl is not, however, entirely convincing and anyway does nothing to deflect blame away from Suffolk and Somerset. While the spoiling tactics of these noblemen may well have exacerbated tensions, the root cause of the failure of the Addled Parliament remained money. James was desperate for financial assistance but, like their predecessors in the first parliament of the reign, the members of the Commons in 1614 were united in their refusal to grant the sums necessary to provide the crown with a secure financial base.

As a direct result of the outbreak of a major European war in 1618, the last two parliaments of James's reign were dominated by considerations of foreign policy. James called a parliament at the beginning of 1621 to back up his public commitment to go to war to recover the Palatinate which had been invaded by Spanish troops the previous summer. The MPs responded quickly by offering him two subsidies and then proceeded to launch a full-scale assault upon monopolists – wealthy businessmen who had purchased from the crown the sole right to manufacture certain basic commodities and who were thus able to sell inferior products at inflated prices without fear of competition from rival products. The attack on this grievance led to criminal charges being brought against the notorious monopolists Sir Giles Mompesson and Sir Francis Michell, and culminated in the impeachment of the lord chancellor, Francis Bacon. James allowed the Commons their head in these proceedings and the MPs left for their long summer recess on relatively good terms with him. When they re-assembled in November, however, any goodwill was soon destroyed by a bitter quarrel over whether the war which James had threatened should now be launched. Over the summer it had become obvious to some MPs that James had been bluffing earlier in the year, that he was still reluctant to go to war, and continued to hope that he could achieve a peaceful solution to the Palatinate crisis through negotiation with the Spanish. When the MPs called for the adoption of the alternative strategy of a naval war against Spain and the termination of the marriage negotiations with Madrid, James furiously reminded them that they had no right to discuss foreign policy and further claimed that they held their privileges only by royal favour. The Commons then drew up their famous Protestation, claiming that freedom of speech was 'the ancient and undoubted birthright and inheritance of the subjects of England', and the session ended acrimoniously with an angry James ripping the Protestation out of the Commons' journal and imprisoning a number of prominent MPs.

When a new parliament met in February 1624, those in the Commons who were looking for a war against Spain had gained two powerful allies: Prince Charles and the duke of Buckingham. Following their visit to Madrid in 1623 and their failure to bring negotiations for a Spanish marriage to a successful conclusion, Charles and Buckingham had returned to England determined to pressurize James into declaring war on those who had humiliated them. With their encouragement, in March 1624 the Commons called for an immediate declaration of war. When James responded by asking them to find the huge sum of at least one million pounds to finance it, the MPs offered him only £300,000, a figure which appeared extremely generous to them, but which was in reality enough to finance a land war for only a few months. When Lionel Cranfield made known his opposition to the war on the grounds of the harm it would cause to the royal finances, Buckingham removed him from the scene by organizing his impeachment by parliament. The MPs left Westminster in May 1624 in good heart following the enactment of their subsidy bill, but, despite the strength of the coalition calling for the immediate commencement of hostilities, the war they had voted for did not materialize until after James's death ten months later.

The attitude of the Commons in 1624 towards the approach of war has been the subject of some debate among historians in recent years. Conrad Russell (1979) has argued that the majority of MPs remained fearful of the increases in taxation that war would bring and preoccupied by the domestic concerns of the areas they represented; in his judgement, they had to be cajoled by Charles and Buckingham into expressing what was at best only lukewarm support for a war. More recently, however, this view has been challenged by Thomas Cogswell (1989a) who has argued that there was widespread support for a war throughout the country and that the Commons joined with their constituents in embracing wholeheartedly the call for hostilities. Russell's case would appear to be strengthened by the failure of the MPs to put their money where their mouths were and provide sufficient funds to wage an effective campaign. It is quite possible, however, that their reluctance to grant the sums James had demanded stemmed not from any lack of enthusiasm for the prospect of a war against Spain but rather from a genuine inability to grasp the fact that, as warfare had become so extraordinarily expensive, such fantastic sums were indeed necessary.

While all four of James's parliaments were marked by tensions, disagreements, and misunderstandings, such problems had characterized parliamentary sessions since their inception and had certainly been evident on many occasions during Elizabeth's reign. Of themselves, they do not provide a compelling reason to conclude that by 1625 crown and parliament had become trapped in a desperate power struggle that would inevitably end in military conflict. Despite his public criticisms of the behaviour of his MPs and his exasperation at their resistance to his policies, James never made any serious attempt to dispense with parliaments for good. On the contrary, he continued to negotiate patiently with successive assemblies over the problematic issues of parliamentary privilege, monopolies, and foreign policy. As a result, as Conrad Russell (1979) remarked at the end of his exhaustive study of the 1621 and 1624 parliaments, at James's death 'not very much was wrong with relations between crown and parliament'.

The real watershed came not in 1603 but in 1625. As Charles I and his MPs locked horns over Buckingham's increased dominance, the disappointing progress of the wars against Spain and France, and above all the advance of Arminianism, the early parliaments of Charles's reign witnessed the rapid breakdown of the working relationship that James had inherited from

Elizabeth and passed on to his son. Within five years, the atmosphere of mutual fear and mistrust had reached such a pitch that the MPs would resort to physical force to delay a dissolution and Charles would vow to rule for as long as he could without calling another parliament. Civil war was by no means inevitable in 1629, but the rapid erosion of trust which had occurred in the short time since Charles's accession had made it a much more real prospect than it had been at the end of James's reign.

5

Foreign policy

Following Martin Luther's challenge to the authority of the Roman Catholic church and the subsequent emergence of Protestantism in Germany and Switzerland during the early sixteenth century, Europe was convulsed by a period of intense religious upheaval. Conflict was temporarily halted by the Peace of Augsburg of 1555, which allowed the German princes to opt for either Catholicism or Lutheranism, but for the next half-century Europe remained in a state of religious cold war, divided into two ideologically opposed armed camps. The principal champions of the resurgent counter-Reformation Catholic church were the Spanish and Austrian Habsburgs, who remained committed to the struggle to destroy both the Lutheran and Calvinist varieties of Protestantism in Germany, Switzerland, and England. While a Europe-wide religious war was avoided during the late sixteenth century, the French state was crippled for forty years by serious internal religious conflict, and after 1566 militant Calvinist rebels in the Netherlands engaged in a long and bitter struggle for independence from Catholic Spain which continued on into the seventeenth century. During the early years of her reign, Elizabeth I attempted to steer a middle course between the hostile religious factions on the continent, but in the 1580s she was sucked into war with Philip II's Spain and in 1588 England only narrowly avoided invasion and occupation by the Spanish. The war between

England and Spain continued during the 1590s and was inherited by James in 1603. The new king, therefore, entered upon a very tense international scene, and one where full-scale religious war remained a very real prospect.

James I's predecessors as English monarchs had long considered foreign affairs to be their royal prerogative – their own special and personal area of responsibility with which their subjects had no right to interfere. James continued this tradition after 1603, pursuing his own personal goals often in the face of considerable opposition from his councillors, MPs, and a wider public opinion. He frequently saw ambassadors from foreign states alone, and at one point he wrote a long poem arguing that: 'no use were made of council tables, if state affairs were public bables'. When the 1621 parliament voiced its opposition to the Spanish marriage, a furious James forbade any further discussion of the matter, and, even when his son and Buckingham joined forces with a large group of MPs in 1624 to demand a war against Spain, James refused to be budged from his own alternative strategy.

James's foreign policy was dominated throughout the reign by the twin aims of keeping England at peace and preventing the emergence of widespread religious conflict in the rest of Europe. Regarding himself as '*Rex Pacificus*' ('the peace-loving king'), he adopted as his motto '*beati pacifici*' ('blessed are the peacemakers') and was fond of quoting the Latin aphorism '*dulce bellum inexpertis*' ('war is only attractive to those who have not experienced it'). Whether this pacific outlook stemmed more from his own personal timidity and aversion to violence, from some ethical objection to warfare, or from an awareness of its damaging political and economic repercussions is difficult to tell. What is clear, however, is that it resulted in a foreign policy whose principal themes were the construction of marriage alliances with both Protestant and Catholic states on the continent, and friendship with the dominant European power, Spain. While this was an approach which was perfectly adapted to the meagre financial resources of the English crown, it was also one which was extremely unpopular with large numbers of James's nationalistic Protestant subjects, who by now considered an intense hatred of Spain to be a core element of their political and religious heritage.

One of the first initiatives to follow James's accession was the ending of the Elizabethan war with Spain by the Treaty of London of 1604. While this move was fully in line with the new king's approach to foreign affairs, preparations for peace had in fact been set in motion before 1603 by Robert Cecil, for Cecil was equally suspicious of both Spain and France, which, following the ending of its religious civil wars, was now clearly re-emerging as an international force under the capable king, Henry IV. The other central objective of English diplomacy during the early years of the reign was to prolong the conflict in the Netherlands between the Dutch rebel forces and the Spanish army. Spain's attempt to reduce the resistance of the northern Netherlands' provinces was an enormous drain on its military and financial resources and made it difficult for it to contemplate major offensive action elsewhere in Europe. For these reasons, James and Henry IV conducted a series of negotiations about providing co-ordinated Anglo–French assistance to the rebels. These proved unproductive, and in 1609 the Spanish and Dutch agreed on a twelve-year truce. Maurice Lee (1970) has argued that this development was a major setback for the English and has criticized James for not seeing that it was in his interests to join with France in providing the increased financial support which might have encouraged the Dutch to keep fighting. Whether, however, hostilities would have continued had England provided money and whether any continuation of the Netherlands' rebellion would have prevented the subsequent descent into a more widespread conflict in central Europe can only remain matters for conjecture.

Within a few weeks of the signing of the Truce of Antwerp by Spain and the Dutch in 1609, the death of the duke of Cleves-Jülich led to a succession dispute in Germany which brought the members of the Evangelical (or Protestant) Union to the brink of war with the Austrian Habsburgs and the states of the Catholic League. After the French and Dutch had expressed their willingness to support the Protestant cause in Germany, James too was persuaded to commit several thousand troops to the struggle against the Catholics, and only the assassination of Henry IV in the summer of 1610 prevented a resort to full-scale war. Over the next two years James cemented his links with the Protestant cause on the continent by agreeing to the marriage of his daughter Elizabeth to the leader of the German Protestants, Frederick V of the Palatinate, and by entering into a defensive alliance with the Evangelical Union. In addition, in 1612 he made a public statement of support for the Edict of Nantes which guaranteed freedom of worship for the Huguenots in France.

While these actions were seen by many English men and women as welcome evidence of his desire to make England a leading member of the international Protestant cause, in reality James had at no time deviated from his commitment to the search for compromise and conciliation. His support for the Evangelical Union had been motivated by a desire to counterbalance what he saw as Habsburg aggression in Germany, and he had agreed to the marriage connection with Frederick in the hope that it would provide him with a power base from which he could more effectively work for an end to the cold war between the rival religious blocs and for the securing of a lasting peace. When in 1614 he was able successfully to negotiate a compromise in the second phase of the Cleves-Jülich crisis which followed Spanish military intervention on behalf of the Catholic claimant, James began to believe that he had achieved a unique position as Europe's peace-broker, and this led him to over-estimate his international influence in a way which was to have unfortunate consequences after 1618.

The decision in 1614 to seek a marriage alliance with Catholic Spain as a counterweight to the connection with the Evangelical Union was another logical step in James's quest to maintain the role of international mediator. While the initiative found favour with some of James's advisers, such as the Howards, who sympathized with Catholicism and saw the large dowry which the infanta would bring as the solution to James's endemic financial problems, others in the government with a more staunchly Protestant perspective, in particular Sir Ralph Winwood, Sir Henry Neville, and Henry Wriothesley, earl of Southampton, were implacably opposed to it. As a consequence, over the next few years divergent attitudes to the Spanish match became a central issue in the increasingly bitter faction-fighting at James's court. The logic behind the marriage negotiations was also entirely lost on a wider public opinion in England which was horrified at the prospect of cementing so close a tie with the country's principal religious enemy. None the less, over the next few years negotiations for a marriage between Prince Charles and the Infanta Maria proceeded, albeit at a rather desultory pace, in London and Madrid.

While the main English negotiator in Spain was Sir John Digby, the Spanish entrusted the face-to-face discussions with James to their envoy, Diego Sarmiento de Acuña, count of Gondomar. James soon struck up a close working relationship with this charming, clever, and experienced Spanish nobleman, but those contemporaries and historians who have concluded that he subsequently became the Spaniard's pawn have seriously under-estimated James's own intelligence and diplomatic ability. As C. H. Carter (1964a and 1964b) has conclusively shown, James and Gondomar shared a mutual respect and the same basic approach to international relations, and worked in partnership for a marriage which, despite the misgivings of their more prejudiced and suspicious contemporaries, they genuinely believed would do a great deal to maintain a lasting peace in Europe. Although he was never Gondomar's dupe, James did, none the less, miscalculate over the Spanish match by consistently failing to pay sufficient regard to the alarm that it provoked among his subjects, and by persevering with it long after the outbreak of the Thirty Years War had deprived it of any real diplomatic relevance.

The crisis which plunged Europe into the war that James had long dreaded originated in Bohemia. In 1618 the Bohemian Protestant nobility rose up in revolt against their newly-elected Catholic king, the Habsburg Ferdinand of Styria. The following year, only a few days after Ferdinand had been elected Holy Roman Emperor, they offered their vacant throne to James's Calvinist son-in-law, Frederick of the Palatinate. After seeking James's advice, Frederick proceeded to accept the offer without waiting to hear his father-in-law's views. By taking the Bohemian crown he provoked and insulted Ferdinand in a way that the new emperor could hardly afford to ignore, and the dispute soon escalated into a major conflict between the Catholic and Protestant powers of central Europe. Whilst many in England were delighted by Frederick's willingness to champion the rights of the Bohemian Protestants and to challenge the dominance of the Austrian Habsburgs, James himself was dismayed by his son-in-law's impetuous move, which he realized might wreck all his efforts to woo the Habsburgs in Spain, and he quickly made a public statement dissociating himself from his action.

Frederick enjoyed his new kingdom for little more than a year, for in November 1620 his Bohemian army was crushed by the forces of the German Catholic League under Maximilian of Bavaria at the Battle of the White Mountain near Prague. By this time, too, Frederick had lost his homeland of the Palatinate, which had been invaded both by Catholic League forces and Spanish troops under the command of Spinola. As James had feared, the Spanish Habsburgs had decided to intervene to support the Austrian branch of the family, both because they realized that their fortunes were to a very large degree interdependent and also because by occupying the Lower Palatinate they could safeguard the 'Spanish road' – their supply corridor through Germany which would once again be vital to their military effort if hostilities with the Dutch were to recommence after the end of the twelve years truce in 1621. When news of the Spanish invasion of the Palatinate reached England in September 1620, many in the country were outraged, and Frederick and Elizabeth were soon portrayed as tragic and romantic martyrs for Protestantism. Even the cautious James now felt compelled to come to their aid and he made a pledge that, unless the Palatinate were restored to Frederick, he would go to war in the spring of 1621 to recover it. In order to show he was serious he then summoned the parliament which met at the beginning of 1621, encouraged his subjects to make voluntary contributions towards the costs of the promised war, and supported the raising of a force of English volunteers under the command of Sir Horace Vere.

These initiatives once again led many in England to believe that their king might at last be about to assume his rightful role as military champion of European Protestantism. In reality, however, as during the Cleves-Jülich crisis, James's chief priority remained the search for a peaceful accommodation. His endorsement of Vere had merely been an attempt to appease public opinion, and in calling the 1621 parliament he was only rattling a sabre which he had no intention of dipping in blood. As his MPs discussed how much money they should provide for the coming war, James publicly declared that it would not be fought over religion and privately continued to pursue the Spanish match and to negotiate behind the scenes in the hope that he could persuade the Habsburgs to withdraw from the Palatinate in exchange for Frederick's renunciation of the

Bohemian throne. While this approach possessed some theoretical logic, in practice it was over-ambitious and deeply flawed. James failed to take sufficient account of the fact that Ferdinand had already promised both the Upper Palatinate and Frederick's electoral vote to Maximilian of Bavaria, and he was completely unable to force the obstinate and foolhardy Frederick to give up his claim to the Bohemian crown. The plan was effectively wrecked at the end of the year when James surrendered up all his bargaining power by abruptly dissolving parliament after it had demanded an immediate diversionary war against Spain and the ending of the Anglo–Spanish marriage negotiations. Even then, however, James would not accept that events had overtaken his diplomacy, and throughout 1622 he persisted in his belief that a marriage alliance with Spain offered the best hope for a return to peace in Germany.

The last desperate throw of the dice in this search for peace through marriage was the journey of Charles and Buckingham to Madrid in February 1623. The prince and favourite spent eight months in Spain, but, despite making major concessions over the terms of the marriage treaty, they failed to persuade the Spanish to proceed with the match. On their return to England in the autumn, they were greeted by scenes of wild celebration, which Thomas Cogswell (1989b) has described as 'one of the most impressive displays of popular emotion in the entire seventeenth century'. Anxious to avenge themselves for the humiliation they felt they had suffered in Madrid, Charles and Buckingham now joined forces with those in the country who were pressing for war. They worked closely with the MPs of James's fourth parliament, which met in February 1624, and initiated discussions in Paris aimed at providing Charles with a French bride and enlisting Louis XIII's support for an anti-Habsburg coalition. Although the marriage negotiations were ultimately successful, the French showed no enthusiasm for a military alliance.

The English king, meanwhile, was proving a more substantial obstacle to war than his son and favourite had anticipated. While he was prepared to back military intervention, like that of the German mercenary Count Mansfeld, with the specific and limited aim of the recovery of the Palatinate, James persisted in his steadfast refusal to support a more general war, and Charles, Buckingham, and parliament struggled in vain to pressurize him into a change of heart. Elizabeth of Bohemia was well aware that it was her father who alone stood in the way of English military aid for her husband, and when she received the news of James's death in the spring of 1625 she is said to have remarked: 'Now you may be sure all will go well in England.' Within a few months of his accession, Charles had fulfilled his sister's expectations by declaring war on Spain, and several years later he caused his father to turn in his grave by commencing hostilities against the French too.

By remaining at peace from 1604 to 1625, James achieved one of his major foreign policy objectives. His consistent refusal to involve England in armed conflict in Europe both spared his subjects the considerable social and economic dislocations that warfare would inevitably have brought in its wake, and protected the weak English public finance system from a shock that might well have led to its complete collapse. The policy was, of course, highly unpopular and did drive an unfortunate wedge between James and his subjects, particularly during the last years of the reign. The king and his closest advisers knew, however, that colossal sums of money would be needed if England were to involve itself in a land war on the continent, and they had good reason to doubt whether even the most bellicose elements in the country were prepared to find the enormous financial resources that their preferred policy would necessitate. What is also clear is that many of those who deplored James's commitment to peace had become insulated from the realities of conflict and took the considerable benefits of peace for granted. James was thus quite justified in quoting *dulce bellum inexpertis* at them, and historians should be careful not to give undue weight to what were often naive condemnations of the king's commitment to peace.

James's other objective – to keep Europe free of all-out religious warfare – succeeded up until 1618 but fell apart during the last six years of the reign. Perhaps because of his earlier success as a mediator in 1614, James approached the Bohemian crisis with an inflated view of his own importance and diplomatic ability, and, once the war which he had worked so hard to avoid had become a reality, he consistently failed to realize that there was very little he could do to bring about a negotiated return to peace. He subsequently made a number of diplomatic miscalculations, by far the most serious of which was his obsessive pursuit of the Spanish match well beyond the point where Madrid was genuinely interested in it and it offered any realistic prospect of bringing about an end to the fighting. But even though James's diplomacy during these last years was a clear failure, critics of it should remember that he might have achieved more if others with influence in the various courts of Europe had shared his desire to avoid a damaging conflict, and in particular if his foolish and politically inept son-in-law had followed his advice and abandoned his Bohemian crusade. As Maurice Lee (1990) has commented:

> Historians who criticize King James – and James's tactics if not his objectives are certainly open to question – should in fairness point out that the policies of many of his contemporaries were equally or even more mistaken, and that some of James's errors stemmed from his failure to realize just how stupid some of his contemporaries were.

When James died in 1625 his pacific foreign policy had rendered him an object of vilification to many of his subjects. Within a very short space of time, however, events had done much to vindicate him; for, despite Elizabeth of Bohemia's optimism, all did not subsequently go well in England. The successive military disasters and heightened domestic tensions which followed Charles's entry into the maelstrom of the Thirty Years War had by the end of the 1620s provided eloquent testimony to the fact that it had been James and not his critics who had exhibited the more realistic and hard-headed approach to international affairs.

6

James I and the English church

Although James I was not a conventionally pious man, throughout his life he showed a considerable intellectual interest in
religious issues. A keen amateur theologian, he was the author
of several religious tracts, and taking part in religious disput-
ations was one of his favourite forms of relaxation. On his
accession in 1603, therefore, the English church acquired
probably its most theologically learned supreme governor, and
one who possessed well-informed and forceful views on all the
important religious issues of his day. It also acquired a leader
who was far more enthusiastically Calvinist than his predecessor. James had received an impeccable Calvinist upbringing
in Scotland at the hands of George Buchanan and his other
tutors, and in later life his unequivocal personal commitment to
Calvinist theology was clearly displayed on a number of occasions. He certainly accepted the core Calvinist doctrine of
double predestination, which argued that God had divided
humankind into two immutable groups, one predestined for
heaven, the other predestined for hell. During 1611 and 1612,
he publicly defended this belief in a literary debate with one of
its critics, the Dutchman Conrad Vorstius, and in 1618 he gave
firm instructions to the English representatives who were to
attend the religious conference at Dort in the United Provinces
that they should support the Dutch predestinarian party.

Historians of religion, such as R. T. Kendall (1979) and Peter

Lake (1987), have recently subdivided Calvin's sixteenth- and seventeenth-century English followers into two distinct groups: experimental Calvinists and credal Calvinists. The experimental Calvinists adhered to a strict and literal interpretation of the doctrine of double predestination; they strove to remove all traces of ungodliness from their daily lives and actively sought to distance themselves religiously and socially from the ungodly, or reprobate, majority amongst whom they lived. The great majority of those who have in the past been identified by the older labels of 'puritan' or 'godly' belong to this group. The credal Calvinists were no less committed to Calvinist theology, but in their practical applications of it they were generally less rigid and intense, and they regarded the social teaching of the experimental Calvinists as elitist and sectarian.

According to this useful typology, James I was very clearly a credal Calvinist. Like Elizabeth, he favoured a broad, inclusive church, and he was deeply suspicious of those whose religious beliefs led them to cut themselves off from, or create deep divisions within, their local communities. He had little sympathy with sabbatarianism – the attempt to maintain Sunday, or the Christian sabbath, as a day given over exclusively to public and private religious exercises – and in 1618 he outraged many of his experimental Calvinist subjects by issuing a Book of Sports which gave official encouragement to those who wished to take part in sporting and leisure pursuits after attending Sunday services. He was also well aware that predestination was a difficult doctrine, which could produce damaging social and psychological consequences if incorrectly or inadequately explained to the laity. Thus, the new ecclesiastical canons which he authorized in 1604 described predestination as '[more] fitted for schools and universities than simple auditors [listeners]', and allowed only bishops, deacons, and 'learned men' to discuss it. Another aspect of James's religious outlook which distanced him from many credal Calvinists, as well as all experimental Calvinists, was his broad-minded attitude towards Roman Catholicism. Whereas the great majority of Calvin's followers saw the papacy as the antichristian epitome of evil and regarded Catholics with a pathological fear and loathing, James was much more respectful towards Rome. On one occasion he declared in a letter to Robert Cecil: 'I reverence their church as our Mother Church, although clogged with many infirmities and corruptions.'

54

While James remained firm in his commitment to a credal Calvinist theological position, he was equally unwavering in his repudiation of some of the most important features of Calvinist ecclesiastical organization. Rejecting Calvin's view that the church should be independent of the state and have sole authority over its own affairs, he was determined to retain the Erastian traditions of the English church and to make sure that it remained firmly subordinate to the secular arm of his government. He was also adamantly opposed to presbyterianism, the Genevan model of church government which replaced bishops with a system of elders and synods chosen by grassroots congregations. He claimed that this was a system 'which accordeth as well with monarchy as God with the Devil', and, as he made clear in his famous 'No bishop, no king' comment at the Hampton Court conference, he saw the suppression of episcopacy as a direct precursor of the abolition of monarchy. Whether James ever subscribed to the view held by some of his bishops that episcopacy was *jure divino* ('instituted by divine law') is not clear. He evidently did not support it on these grounds in 1603 and a number of historians have argued that he continued to employ more pragmatic justifications of it throughout the reign. J. P. Somerville (1983), however, has claimed that James was converted to the *jure divino* position some time before 1625. Whether or not he did come to accept it, he was certainly aware that the doctrine was something of a double-edged sword which needed to be handled with great care; for while it gave a greatly enhanced status and authority to the episcopal order, it correspondingly threatened his ability to keep his bishops under tight royal control.

James's policy towards the English church had three major objectives: the maintenance of harmonious relations with its Scottish counterpart, the segregation of its moderate critics from its more extremist opponents, and the preservation of stability through the careful balancing of the Calvinist and Arminian factions within the ranks of the conformist clergy.

With regard to the first of these objectives, James never forgot that developments in one of his national churches had inevitable repercussions in the other, and in his management of the ecclesiastical affairs of both his kingdoms he was anxious to avoid initiatives which might needlessly antagonize religious opinion on the other side of the border. Conrad Russell (1990) has pointed out that for the same reason 'the dominant influence in each church went to those least likely to denounce the arrangements of the other', citing as evidence George Abbot's appointment as archbishop of Canterbury in 1611, which he believes was due primarily to his acceptability to the Scots.

The second central theme of James's management of the church – the attempt to prevent the formation of dangerous alliances between moderates and extremists – is evident in his dealings with both puritans and Roman Catholic recusants. James tackled the serious puritan problem he inherited from Elizabeth by attempting to accommodate the views of those moderate reformers who, though dissatisfied with the state of the English church, were prepared to accept its bishops and to work within the law for its peaceful reform, whilst at the same time vigorously hounding the small presbyterian minority which was actively seeking the total destruction of the religious status quo. The aim was to prevent those in the former group, whom Robert Cecil referred to as 'religious men of moderate spirits', from becoming subverted by what he called 'the turbulent humours of some that dream of nothing but a new hierarchy'. The English puritan movement had high expectations of James I in 1603. Many of its members believed that their new Calvinist governor would move quickly to cleanse his church of the ceremonial remnants of popery to which the old queen had remained stubbornly attached, and that he would inaugurate a programme of reform which would improve the quality of the clergy and make better provision for the preaching of God's Word throughout the country. Although in the short term these hopes were to be seriously disappointed, by the second half of the reign most moderate puritans were more fully integrated into the established church than at any time since Elizabeth's repudiation of Archbishop Edmund Grindal in 1576.

On his journey south in 1603 James was presented with the Millenary Petition for church reform, which had apparently been signed by a thousand puritan ministers. The measures it advocated included the removing from the liturgy of a number of popish practices, including the signing of the cross in baptism, the easing of official pressure for the wearing of the surplice, and initiatives to deal with the problems of pluralism, non-residence, and inadequate clerical stipends. James responded to this appeal by summoning several of his bishops and representatives of the puritan petitioners to a religious conference held at Hampton Court in early 1604. According to an older historical tradition, the Hampton Court Conference broke up in complete disarray after one of the puritan delegates had aroused James's anger by referring sympathetically to presbyterianism. In the early 1960s, however, Mark Curtis (1961) demonstrated that the conference itself had been reasonably harmonious and productive, and that James had distanced himself from his bishops and given the puritan position genuine consideration. According to Curtis, the puritans left Hampton Court at the conclusion of the debate very satisfied with what they had achieved and convinced that James was committed to reforming the church by ending pluralism and disseminating a preaching ministry more widely across the country. The fact that such reforms did not materialize was, in Curtis's view, the fault not of James but of his leading bishops who worked hard in the months following the conference to nullify its recommendations. Although Curtis's picture of what happened at Hampton Court is still generally accepted as accurate, several historians have suggested that it should be modified slightly. Frederick Shriver (1982) has argued that James was not as detached from his bishops as Curtis claimed, and Patrick Collinson (1983) has concluded that the king deserves some criticism for allowing them to obstruct the implementation of the conference's decisions.

If Hampton Court was a disappointment for the puritan movement, James's elevation of Richard Bancroft to the see of Canterbury just a few months later appeared an even crueller blow. Bancroft was a conservative cleric, very much in the mould of his predecessor John Whitgift, who had little sympathy with the outlook of even the most moderate reformers. Soon after taking office, he mounted a vigorous campaign to force the clergy to conform to the new ecclesiastical canons of 1604, which demanded they accept every part of the Book of Common Prayer and every one of the Thirty-Nine Articles. They were now required to wear the surplice for all services, to retain the sign of the cross in baptism, and to demand that their parishioners receive communion kneeling.

Several years into the reign, therefore, English puritans could have been forgiven for concluding that, in believing that James would prove more sympathetic towards them than Elizabeth, they had been sadly mistaken. These early setbacks were, however, deceptive. At Hampton Court James had shown himself to be far less hostile to puritanism than his bishops were, and he had chosen Bancroft to succeed Whitgift only after some hesitation, and because he was the obvious and the strongest candidate, rather than because of his conservative views. Furthermore, he did not share Bancroft's enthusiasm for a violent purge of those clergymen who would not accept the canons. In the event, only around eighty ministers – or less than one per cent of English parish clergy – lost their livings as a result of the archbishop's campaign, and some ministers escaped deprivation even though they refused to conform in any way. No further ejections of clergy took place after 1606, and when Bancroft died in 1610 James replaced him with the committed evangelical Calvinist, George Abbot. Abbot shared many of the religious views of the moderate puritans and was unwilling to discipline those who objected to the more 'popish' aspects of the church's liturgy. Similarly, because he placed great stress on the need for an effective preaching ministry, he was reluctant to persecute puritan ministers – whom he considered to be among the best preachers in the church – simply because they refused to conform to his predecessor's ceremonial injunctions. As Kenneth Fincham (1988) has shown, over the next ten years Abbot co-operated closely with James in a policy of tolerance towards moderate episcopalian puritans and vigorous harassment of presbyterians. As a result the English church enjoyed more tranquillity than at any time since the Reformation.

The same conciliatory approach was taken towards the Roman Catholic community. The great majority of Catholics consistently ignored the laws requiring them to attend Protestant Sunday services; as a result they were classified as 'recusants' and forced to pay heavy recusancy fines for their non-attendance. There were around 35,000 Roman Catholic recusants in England in 1603 – slightly more than one per cent of the total population. Most of them were thoroughly reconciled to the reality of a Protestant monarchy, and consistently ignored papal directives calling upon them to renounce their allegiance to the state and actively to plot for its destruction. Much to the consternation and alarm of his Protestant subjects, James was inclined to turn a blind eye to the religious practices of these loyal recusants so long as they were discreet; he was even prepared to allow church-papists, like the earl of North-ampton, who participated in Protestant services as well as attending private Catholic masses, to rise to very prominent positions within his government. Once again the aim of this lenient approach was to detach moderate Catholic opinion from a small revolutionary minority, which included those involved in the 1603 Bye Plot and the 1605 Gunpowder Plot. At one time historians saw these Catholic conspiracies to depose James as evidence of a general disenchantment within the recusant community over James's actions during the first two years of his reign. The Bye Plot was probably the pro-duct of Catholic disappointment at James's early decision to continue to levy recusancy fines. Jenny Wormald (1985), how-ever, has argued convincingly that many of those implicated in the 1605 plot to assassinate James at the state opening of parliament had been involved in schemes to bring about a Spanish succession for some years prior to Elizabeth's death, and had turned to gunpowder in 1605 as their last desperate chance to achieve a goal they had been pursuing for at least seven years.

The discovery of the plot was quickly followed by the enactment of several new penal laws against Catholics, but these do not appear to have been enforced with any real vigour, and, perhaps surprisingly, James himself was not diverted from his remarkably open-minded approach to the Catholic com-munity. He continued to regard recusancy as primarily a political rather than a religious problem, and in 1606 he devised a special oath of allegiance and tacitly offered to leave un-molested those Catholics who would swear their loyalty to him and pay their recusancy fines. The papacy, of course, refused to recognize the validity of this oath and James subsequently became involved in a heated literary debate on its merits with the Catholic theologian, Cardinal Bellarmine. Although the oath was only sporadically administered during the rest of the reign, the king continued to regard it as an important litmus test of Catholic loyalty. Thus, as Kenneth Fincham and Peter Lake (1985) have pointed out, although James could not grant the recusant community 'toleration', he did offer moderate and loyal Catholics 'tolerance'. As a direct consequence, they en-joyed a more congenial environment within which to practise their proscribed beliefs than they had under Elizabeth, and, despite the suspicions of their Protestant neighbours, they had little incentive to seek to change the regime.

The third element in James's search for religious stability was his studious balancing of the various factions within the ranks of the conformist clergy. This was achieved principally through the careful selection and control of the episcopal bench. During the course of the reign James raised to the rank of bishop a number of highly committed Calvinists like George Abbot, John King, James Montagu, and Arthur Lake. These clerics regarded themselves primarily as pastors, and considered the evangelizing of the nation through the provision of more preaching to be one of their chief priorities. James also, however, elevated a number of more conservative, 'Arminian' figures like Richard Neile, Lancelot Andrewes, John Buckeridge, Gilbert Overall, and William Laud; these bishops did not share their Calvinist colleagues' enthusiasm for preaching and saw themselves first and foremost as the guardians of order, decorum, and discipline in the church.

The Arminian bishops represented the small group of English clerics who sympathized with the doctrinal teaching of the Dutch theologian, Jacob Arminius. Although Arminius was a Protestant, he rejected the more rigid applications of the Calvinist doctrine of double predestination and, like Roman Catholics, he stressed instead the importance of good works in the process of achieving salvation. His theological opinions had precipitated a major religious and political crisis within the United Provinces, which was eventually resolved in favour of the predestinarians by the Synod of Dort in 1619. The English Arminians shared Arminius's deep misgivings about the doctrine of double predestination, an outlook which placed them firmly outside the Calvinist theological consensus which had prevailed in England since 1560. They further antagonized their English Calvinist contemporaries by their support for popish liturgical practices – such as bowing, genuflection, and the use of the sign of the cross – and by their desire to decorate the plain interiors of the English parish churches by re-introducing the pictures, statues, stained glass, and altars, which had been removed after the Reformation and which were widely regarded by Calvinists as idolatrous.

Some historians have suggested that James promoted the Arminians because he was won over to their theological views.

Nicholas Tyacke (1987), in particular, has argued that James was beginning to experience real doubts about predestination in the last years of his life, citing as evidence the growing influence of the Arminian faction in the early 1620s and the king's failure to suppress Richard Montagu's inflammatory anti-predestinarian tract, *A New Gag for an Old Goose*, which was published in 1624. There is, however, no reason to believe that James had been converted to the anti-predestinarian views of the Arminians, or that he had promoted these men to the episcopal bench out of any sympathy with their views on salvation. On the contrary, he expressly instructed Bishop Andrewes to keep his reservations about predestination strictly to himself. He wanted the Arminians within the ranks of the bishops because they were prepared to offer him support on issues like the royal supremacy, the liturgy, and foreign policy, and thus provided him with a valuable counterweight to his more acerbic Calvinist bishops, who frequently opposed him over these issues. If the Arminian faction had temporarily gained the upper hand during the last few years of the reign, it was not as a result of any change of heart by James but because the Calvinist bishops John King and James Montagu had both recently died, and Abbot had been forced into retirement following his accidental killing of a gamekeeper whilst hunting in 1621. Even at this late stage James showed his desire to preserve a balance between the various factions by appointing as bishop of Lincoln the Calvinist John Williams.

James's willingness to make use of talented individuals from across the ecclesiastical spectrum allowed him to put together an exceptionally able and conscientious episcopal bench. Some years ago Hugh Trevor-Roper was extremely scathing about the quality of the Jacobean bishops, denouncing them as 'indifferent', 'negligent', and 'secular'. More recently, however, their reputation has been much repaired, and the work of Kenneth Fincham (1990) in particular has revealed that many of James's bishops were men of a very high calibre. Fincham has demonstrated that the majority of them were learned and conscientious clerics who showed great commitment and diligence both in carrying out their responsibilities within their dioceses and in making sure that the interests of the church were represented in the corridors of power. They also contributed substantially to the steady improvement in the quality of the parish clergy. By the end of James's reign most of the local clergy were highly educated professional men, who enjoyed the confidence and respect of their congregations. In 1621 one MP declared in the House of Commons: 'I speak it confidently there were never better ministers since this kingdom stood'; and three years later Bishop Joseph Hall described the parish clergy as '*stupor mundi*' ('the wonder of the world').

In the period up until 1618 James's religious policy was an unqualified success. The king's careful religious diplomacy had promoted the growth of what Patrick Collinson (1983) has called a 'rising tide of consensual, evangelical Calvinism', which had 'all but submerged the old differences between conformity and non-conformity'. The outbreak of full-scale religious war in Europe after 1618 was to impose some serious strains on the policy. It was, for example, directly responsible for causing an unfortunate breach between James and Abbot, who antagonized his master by his strong support for active intervention on behalf of the Protestant cause and his extreme hostility to a Spanish marriage. It also left James more dependent than he would have liked on the Arminians, who shared his reluctance to commit England more fully to the support of continental Protestantism.

But while the Thirty Years War undoubtedly dented James's religious strategy, it did not completely derail it. Although very many English men and women became increasingly worried after 1618 about the fate of their co-religionists on the continent, while James lived very few of them were unduly perturbed about the state of their domestic church. James had steered that church around the various hazards that threatened its well-being with great success, and as Kenneth Fincham and Peter Lake (1985) have remarked: 'it is difficult not to be impressed by the skill with which he handled both anti-Puritan and anti-papal stereotypes to create the ideological space within which the royal will could maneuver and policy be formulated'. Taken together, the maintenance of cordial relations between the English and Scottish churches, the accommodation of puritan and Catholic moderates, and the counterbalancing of the Arminian and Calvinist clerical pressure groups represent a formidable achievement.

It was, however, an achievement that James's successor, Charles, was to overturn very rapidly by repudiating his father's policy of balance and allowing the Arminians to assume a complete dominance of the English episcopal bench by 1633. In 1626 the committed puritan Francis Rous dedicated his anti-Arminian tract, *Testis Veritatis*, to James I, and by 1629 he and a great many of his fellow puritans had begun to look back on James's reign as a lost age of religious harmony. If Charles had had the sense to persevere with his father's ecclesiastical policy of divide and rule, and if he had chosen the pragmatic Calvinist, John Williams, rather than the splenetic Arminian, William Laud, to succeed Abbot as archbishop of Canterbury, his reign might well not have ended in civil war and regicide.

Conclusion

There can be no doubt that James I possessed some major shortcomings as a ruler, the most damaging of which were his over-reliance on favourites, his complete neglect of his public image, and his inability to live within his financial means. His fondness for successive male favourites, and in particular the duke of Buckingham, had by the end of the reign seriously distorted the normal operation of the patronage system and left many important figures both inside and outside the royal court feeling great resentment towards his government. His failure to see the vital importance of maintaining the positive image of monarchy that Elizabeth had worked so hard to create was another grave fault. By presenting himself to his subjects 'warts and all', shorn of the mystique of majesty with which Elizabeth had surrounded herself, James initiated a process which began to erode away the respectful and deferential attitudes of the English people towards the monarchy. Similarly, by presiding over a court which was widely viewed as corrupt and depraved, he allowed himself to become closely associated with behaviour that deeply offended many of his subjects. Between 1603 and 1625 a wide chasm opened up between the cultural and moral values of the court and those of the provincial nation, and the English people became alienated from their sovereign in a way that Elizabeth would never have tolerated. James's greatest defect as a ruler was, however, his extravagance. The charge of persistent and gross over-spending is one from which not even the most sympathetic historian can exonerate him. The enormous waste of financial resources crippled every aspect of government, and doomed to failure all attempts by his ministers to persuade the nation that the crown could no longer adequately perform its functions without regular and substantially increased funding.

It would, however, be a mistake to suggest that James's statecraft was completely without redeeming features. While he had plenty of disagreements with his parliaments, he continued to search for accommodations with his frequently ill-informed and unreasonable MPs, and he never succumbed to the temptation to dispense with their services altogether. As a result, the working relationships he established with his parliaments were not markedly less productive than those Elizabeth had enjoyed with hers, and there is certainly no reason to believe that by 1625 crown and parliament were set on a collision course which would inevitably lead to violent conflict.

The issue that caused the most animosity in the last two parliaments of the reign was, of course, James's foreign policy. His approach here was without question by the end of the reign both intensely unpopular and increasingly unrealistic. Many English men and women were deeply concerned for the survival of Protestantism in Europe, and they found James's refusal to take up arms on behalf of his co-religionists and his persistence with the scheme for a Spanish match both incomprehensible and offensive. It is also clear that by the end of 1621 all prospect of a negotiated peace brokered by James had vanished. On the other hand, James did spare his subjects the trauma of a major conflict, and his suspicion that they had little real idea of what a war would cost and would lose their enthusiasm for it once they began to experience its less agreeable repercussions was to be proved well-founded by the disastrous events that followed his death. For this reason, those who have condemned his foreign policy out of hand have judged James too harshly; it might be fairer to conclude that both the king and his MPs were the hapless victims of developments on the continent over which none of them had much control.

No such equivocation, however, need detract from James's success in the religious sphere. After inheriting from Elizabeth a broad, but tense and divided, church, he preserved its wide boundaries and restored it to peace by negotiating skilfully with the various religious interest groups both inside it and on its fringes. During the second half of the reign, he presided over what within a few years of his death was seen as a halcyon period for the English church, and it is no exaggeration to claim that he effectively solved the puritan problem which had bedevilled religious affairs in England throughout the second half of the sixteenth century. If this achievement has not been as widely recognized as it should have been, it is because it was so quickly turned to dust by his son in the late 1620s.

James I's record as English king was, therefore, a mixed one. He was emphatically not, however, the total disaster that is found in the pages of the Whig histories, and there is no reason to suppose that England was plunging headlong towards civil war in 1625. The real culprit who deserves to carry most of the blame for the catastrophes of the 1640s and 1650s was not James but his far less able successor, Charles. Charles I was to lead his people into a series of wartime humiliations, to resolve publicly to dispense with the English parliament, and above all to support a fatal Arminian take-over of the English church. He has avoided full censure for these actions for so long only because the sins of the son were visited upon the father by historians who found a drunken, homosexual spendthrift a more appropriate scapegoat than a refined and dignified paragon of traditional family life. James I may have been an unattractive man, but he was also a shrewd, capable, and moderately successful ruler and, as Bishop Hacket remarked at the end of the seventeenth century, those who have argued that the English civil war became inevitable during the course of his reign have made the mistake of indulging in 'long spun deductions'.

Select bibliography

Simon Adams, 'Spain or the Netherlands?: The Dilemmas of Early Stuart Foreign Policy', in H. Tomlinson (ed.), *Before the English Civil War* (London, 1983)

C. H. Carter, *The Secret Diplomacy of the Hapsburgs 1585–1624* (New York, 1964a)

C. H. Carter, 'Gondomar: Ambassador to James I', *Historical Journal*, vol. 7 (1964b)

Thomas Cogswell, *The Blessed Revolution: English Politics and the Coming of War 1621–1624* (Cambridge, 1989a)

Thomas Cogswell, 'England and the Spanish Match', in Richard Cust and Ann Hughes (eds), *Conflict in Early Stuart England* (London, 1989b)

Patrick Collinson, 'The Jacobean Religious Settlement: The Hampton Court Conference', in H. Tomlinson (ed.), *Before the English Civil War* (London, 1983)

Pauline Croft 'Robert Cecil and the Early Jacobean Court', in Linda Levy Peck (ed.), *The Mental World of the Jacobean Court* (Cambridge, 1991)

Neil Cuddy, 'The Revival of the Entourage: The Bedchamber of James I 1603–1625', in D. Starkey (ed.), *The English Court from the Wars of the Roses to the Civil War* (London, 1987)

Mark H. Curtis, 'The Hampton Court Conference and its Aftermath', *History*, vol. 46 (1961)

Richard Cust, 'Politics and the Electorate in the 1620s', in Richard Cust and Ann Hughes (eds), *Conflict in Early Stuart England* (London, 1989a)

Richard Cust and Ann Hughes, 'Introduction: After Revisionism', in Richard Cust and Ann Hughes (eds), *Conflict in Early Stuart England* (London, 1989b)

G. Donaldson, *Scotland: James V – James VII* (Edinburgh, 1965)

Kenneth Fincham, 'Prelacy and Politics: Archbishop Abbot's Defence of Protestant Orthodoxy', *Historical Research*, vol. 61 (1988)

Kenneth Fincham, *Prelate as Pastor: The Episcopate of James I* (Oxford, 1990)

Kenneth Fincham and Peter Lake, 'The Ecclesiastical Policy of King James I', *Journal of British Studies*, vol. 24 (1985)

S. R. Gardiner, *The History of England 1603–1642* (10 vols, London, 1883–4)

S. J. Houston, *James I* (London, 1973)

Ann Hughes, *The Causes of the English Civil War* (London, 1991)

R. T. Kendall, *Calvin and English Calvinism to 1649* (Oxford, 1979)

Peter Lake, 'Calvinism and the English Church', *Past and Present*, vol. 114 (1987)

Maurice Lee Jun., *James I and Henry IV: An Essay in English Foreign Policy 1603–1610* (Urbana, 1970)

Maurice Lee Jun., *Great Britain's Solomon: James VI and I in his Three Kingdoms* (Urbana and Chicago, 1990)

Roger Lockyer, *Buckingham* (London, 1981)

R. C. Munden, 'James I and "the growth of mutual mistrust": King, Commons, and Reform, 1603–1604', in Kevin Sharpe (ed.), *Faction and Parliament: Essays on Early Stuart History* (London, 1978a)

R. C. Munden, 'The Defeat of Sir John Fortescue: Court and Country at the Hustings', *English Historical Review*, vol. 93 (1978b)

W. Notestein, *The House of Commons 1604–1610* (London, 1971)

Linda Levy Peck, 'The Earl of Northampton, Merchant Grievances, and the Addled Parliament of 1614', *Historical Journal*, vol. 24 (1981)

Linda Levy Peck, *Northampton: Patronage and Policy at the Court of James I* (London, 1982)

Linda Levy Peck, '"For a king not to be bountiful were a fault": Perspectives on Court Patronage in Early Stuart England', *Journal of British Studies*, vol. 25 (1986)

Conrad Russell, 'Parliamentary History in Perspective 1604–1629', *History*, vol. 61 (1976)

Conrad Russell, *Parliaments and English Politics 1621–1629* (Oxford, 1979)

Conrad Russell, 'The Nature of a Parliament in Early Stuart England', in H. Tomlinson (ed.), *Before the English Civil War* (London, 1983)

Conrad Russell, *The Causes of the English Civil War* (Oxford, 1990)

Conrad Russell, *The Addled Parliament of 1614: The Limits of Revisionism* (Reading, 1992)

Kevin Sharpe, 'Introduction: Parliamentary History 1603–1629: In or Out of Perspective?', in Kevin Sharpe (ed.), *Faction and Parliament: Essays on Early Stuart History* (London, 1978)

Kevin Sharpe, '"Revisionism" Revisited', in Kevin Sharpe (ed.), *Faction and Parliament: Essays on Early Stuart History* (London, 1985 edn)

Kevin Sharpe, 'Crown, Parliament and Locality: Government and

Community in Early Stuart England', *English Historical Review*, vol. 101 (1986)

Frederick Shriver, 'Hampton Court Re-visited: James I and the Puritans', *Journal of Ecclesiastical History*, vol. 33 (1982)

Alan G. R. Smith, 'Introduction', in Alan G. R. Smith (ed.), *The Reign of James VI and I* (London, 1973)

Alan G. R. Smith, 'Constitutional Ideas and Parliamentary Developments in England 1603–1625', in Alan G. R. Smith (ed.), *The Reign of James VI and I* (London, 1973)

J. P. Somerville 'The Royal Supremacy and Episcopacy "Jure Divino" 1603–40', *Journal of Ecclesiastical History*, vol. 34 (1983)

Lawrence Stone, *The Crisis of the Aristocracy 1558–1641* (Oxford, 1965)

Lawrence Stone, *The Causes of the English Revolution* (London, 1972)

Nicholas Tyacke, *Anti-Calvinists: The Rise of English Arminianism c. 1590–1640* (Oxford, 1987)

D. H. Willson, *James VI and I* (London, 1956)

Jenny Wormald, *Court, Kirk and Community: Scotland 1470–1625* (London, 1981)

Jenny Wormald, 'James VI and I: Two Kings or One?', *History*, vol. 68 (1983)

Jenny Wormald, 'Gunpowder, Treason and Scots', *Journal of British Studies*, vol. 24 (1985)